COUNTRIES OF THE WORLD

Myanmar

Gareth Stevens Publishing
MILWAUKEE

About the Author: Pauline Khng obtained her masters degree from the School of Oriental and African Studies, University of London. She has worked as a journalist and editor in Singapore, Hong Kong, and London. She is currently a Research Associate at the Centre for South-East Asian Studies, University of Hull.

Acknowledgments: The author is indebted to numerous friends and acquaintances for their unstinting help, including Anna Allott, Ben Burt, Mary Cameron, Patricia Herbert, Nicholas Martland, Daw May Kyi Win, John Okell, Sayadaw U Pyinnya Thiha, Daw Tin Tin Myaing, the late Professor Mya Maung, and Melanie Maung.

PICTURE CREDITS
Archive Photos: 17, 76, 77, 78, 80
Bes Stock: 5, 20, 21 (top), 24, 34, 54, 55, 66, 74
Michele Burgess: 3 (center), 62
Ben Burt: 36 (top), 51
Focus Team — Italy: 22, 33, 46, 47 (right), 65
Hans Hayden: 71
HBL Network Photo Agency: 68, 69
Renata Holzbachová/Philippe Bénet: 21 (bottom), 29, 32 (top), 37, 64, 89
Ingrid Horstmann: 18, 70, 90 (both)
Dave G. Houser: 10, 16, 19
The Hutchison Library: 26, 38, 72, 73
John R. Jones: 39
Richard I'Anson: 25, 27, 32 (bottom), 40
Melanie Maung: 83
North Wind Picture Archives: 12
Christine Osborne Pictures: 41
Photobank Photolibrary: 36 (bottom), 58, 67, 87, 91
Pietro Scozzari: 2, 3 (bottom), 28, 30, 31, 42, 43, 44, 45, 48, 49, 50, 52, 60, 61
David Simson: 3 (top), 9 (both)
Tan Chung Lee: 7, 57
Liba Taylor Photography: 23
Sayadaw U Pyinnya Thiha: 84, 85
Times Editions: 14, 35
Topham Picturepoint: 4, 8, 11, 13, 15 (top), 15 (center), 59, 79, 81, 82
Vision Photo Agency: 75
Alison Wright: cover, 6, 15 (bottom), 47 (left), 53, 56, 63

Digital Scanning by Superskill Graphics Pte Ltd

Written by
PAULINE KHNG

Edited by
KAREN KWEK

Designed by
LOO CHUAN MING

Picture research by
SUSAN JANE MANUEL

First published in North America in 2000 by
Gareth Stevens Publishing
1555 North RiverCenter Drive, Suite 201
Milwaukee, Wisconsin 53212 USA

For a free color catalog describing
Gareth Stevens' list of high-quality books
and multimedia programs, call
1-800-542-2595 (USA) or
1-800-461-9120 (CANADA).
Gareth Stevens Publishing's
Fax: (414) 225-0377.

© **TIMES EDITIONS PTE LTD 2000**
Originated and designed by
Times Editions Pte Ltd
Times Centre, 1 New Industrial Road
Singapore 536196
http://www.timesone.com.sg/te

Library of Congress Cataloging-in-Publication Data
Khng, Pauline.
Myanmar / by Pauline Khng.
p.   cm. -- (Countries of the world)
Includes bibliographical references and index.
Summary: An overview of the country of Myanmar, formerly known as Burma, that includes information on geography, history, government, lifestyles, language, art, food, and current issues.
ISBN 0-8368-2320-6 (lib. bdg.)
1. Burma--Juvenile literature. [1. Burma]
I. Title. II. Series: Countries of the world (Milwaukee, Wis.)
DS527.4.K45   2000
959.1--dc21   99-39251

Printed in Malaysia

1 2 3 4 5 6 7 8 9 04 03 02 01 00

Contents

AN OVERVIEW OF MYANMAR

Myanmar is a land of gorgeous landscapes, colorful markets, and bustling tea shops. Recent headlines, however, have focused on the country's ongoing political troubles — Myanmar's military regime has been criticized for its harsh treatment of political dissidents and minority groups.

In 1989, the country's official name was changed from *The Socialist Republic of the Union of Burma* to *The Union of Myanmar*. In the Burmese language, the land has been known as *Mranma Prañ*, or *Myanmar*, for several hundred years. Except where territories in the time of British rule are discussed, this text uses the official Burmese names of all territories, with their former English names in parentheses at the first mention.

Opposite: **Villagers go about their daily activities along a canal that leads to Inle Lake, in Shan state.**

Below: **Two boys sit on the steps of the Shwesandaw Pagoda in Bagan (Pagan).**

THE FLAG OF MYANMAR

The current flag of Myanmar was adopted in 1974, when the military regime changed the country's name from *The Union of Burma* to *The Socialist Republic of the Union of Burma.* The flag consists of a blue rectangle on a red background. The color blue represents peace and stability, while red stands for courage and determination. The rice plant and the cogwheel represent, respectively, agriculture and industry, the pillars of Myanmar's economy. Surrounding the rice plant and cogwheel are fourteen stars, one for each of the country's seven states and seven divisions.

Geography

Located in Southeast Asia, Myanmar covers an area of 261,228 square miles (676,580 square kilometers). It shares borders with India and Bangladesh to the west, China to the north, and Laos and Thailand to the east. Myanmar's territory is shaped like a kite, with a long, tapering southern coastal strip facing the Andaman Sea. From north to south, the country spans about 1,275 miles (2,052 km).

Mountains and Plains

Myanmar's heartland is a central plain flanked by the Shan Plateau to the east and mountains to the north and west. Coastal plains lie to the south and southwest of the central plain.

Widely regarded as the cradle of Burmese civilization, the central plain once supported the majority of Myanmar's royal capitals, including Bagan, Inwa (Ava), and Mandalay. Also known as the *dry zone*, the central plain receives very little rainfall. Crops grown there include millet, sesame, and irrigated rice. About half of the population of Myanmar is concentrated farther south, in

INLE LAKE

From floating markets to one-legged rowing races, Inle Lake, in Shan state, is one of Myanmar's major attractions.
(*A Closer Look, page 56*)

Below: **A temple sits atop Mount Popa, the core of an extinct volcano in central Myanmar.**

the delta area of the Ayeyarwady (Irrawaddy) River. Few people inhabit the mountainous areas that cover half the country. The northern mountains form a complex of ranges, with Mount Hkakabo Razi, Myanmar's highest peak, rising to 19,295 feet (5,881 meters). The western ranges include the Rahkine Yoma and extend northward, through the Chin Hills and the Naga Hills, along the border with India. The Shan Plateau in eastern Myanmar has an average elevation of 3,000 feet (914 m) and was formed between 245 million and 66 million years ago.

Myanmar has two strips of coastal land, the southwestern Rahkine coast and the Taninthayi coast in the far south. These areas receive very heavy rainfall, making them ideal for growing rice and a variety of tropical fruits. The division of Bago also forms part of the southern coastline. From the Ayeyarwady delta, the ports of Yangon (Rangoon) and Pathein (Bassein) look out across the Andaman Sea. Myanmar's longest river, the Thanlwin (Salween), flows into the Shan Plateau from the Himalayas and empties into the Gulf of Mottama (Gulf of Martaban).

Above: **Life is simple on the rural outskirts of Pyi (Prome), a town in Bago division.**

RIVER OF REFRESHMENT

Myanmar's rivers have been used to transport people and goods for hundreds of years. The country's main waterway, the Ayeyarwady, begins in the Himalayas and courses about 1,300 miles (2,092 km) across the country, ending in nine mouths in the fertile delta basin.

(A Closer Look, page 64)

Climate

Myanmar has monsoon seasons. The wet period stretches from
May to late October. During this time, strong winds blow into
Myanmar from the southwest, bringing thunderstorms with
heavy rain almost every day. Western Rahkine, southern
Bago, Ayeyarwady, and the Taninthayi coast receive about
120–200 inches (3,048–5,080 millimeters) of rainfall a year. The
central plain, however, surrounded by mountains, receives only
about 20–40 inches (508–1,016 mm) annually. During the cool, dry
season, which lasts from November to February, temperatures
average about 70–80° Fahrenheit (21–27° Celsius). The hottest and
driest months are March and April, when humidity is high and
temperatures may exceed 110° F (43° C). Myanmar's climate
also varies with altitude. Highland areas experience cooler
temperatures — the northern mountain peaks even see snow
between November and January.

Tropical and Temperate Forests

Because Myanmar spans about seventeen degrees of latitude,
its natural vegetation varies from tropical rain forest in the wet,
southern parts to temperate forest in the northern and highland

Above: **Flooded rice
fields adjoin villages
on the Shan Plateau.
Because of its altitude,
this region is cooler
than central Myanmar,
with an average
temperature of 71° F
(22° C). Shan state
receives 75–80 inches
(1,905–2,032 mm) of
rainfall every year.**

areas. Valuable hardwood trees, such as teak, grow on the Bago Yoma range. Mangrove swamps line the coast. Oaks and conifers grow on mountain slopes at altitudes above 3,000 feet (914 m). Rhododendrons, magnolias, and maples thrive in the northern highlands.

Abundant Wildlife

Myanmar's many animals include tigers, bears, wild boars, deer, tapir, and mongooses. Elephants — widely used for transportation in the past — are sometimes used to carry logs today. Myanmar is home to many poisonous snakes, such as the king cobra and several kinds of vipers.

Mynahs, sparrows, crows, and red-whiskered bulbuls are among the many bird species that nest in Myanmar. Flocks of white egrets are commonly seen standing in the paddy (wet rice) fields. Woodpeckers help preserve the teak forests by eating the bee-hole borer insects that attack trees. Weaverbirds got their name because they weave strips of grass into elongated nests that hang from palm trees or roof beams. Myanmar's bird population also includes fish owls and hornbills.

Above: Lotus plants, with their distinctive circular leaves and large, delicate flowers, are a common sight in Myanmar.

Left: The great hornbill is a rare bird that lives in the forests of Myanmar and Thailand. The slow disappearance of its natural habitat is threatening its survival in the wild.

VANISHING FORESTS

Myanmar is the world's biggest producer of teak. Now, the country's valuable hardwood forests are dwindling, resulting in both a loss of animal habitat and other environmental problems.
(A Closer Look, page 70)

9

History

Early peoples are believed to have settled in the Ayeyarwady river basin and on its delta about 11,000 years ago. Archaeological finds indicate that they used stone and wooden tools, much like the early civilizations that appeared in other parts of Southeast Asia during the same period.

According to Chinese records from the Tang Dynasty, the Pyu, an ethnic group that spoke Tibeto-Burman languages, established city-kingdoms in areas north of the Ayeyarwady delta between the first century B.C. and A.D. 800. A sophisticated and cultured people, the Pyu created new trade routes and built grand Buddhist temples.

BAGAN'S ANCIENT SPLENDOR

Sprawling over a vast area on the eastern bank of the Ayeyarwady River are the temple monuments to an extraordinary civilization. (*A Closer Look, page 44*)

Above: **Bagan was the capital of an empire that flourished between the ninth and thirteenth centuries.**

The kingdom of an Austro-Asian group known as the Mon developed south of the Pyu civilization. The Mon gradually became one of the most advanced peoples in the region. They spread their culture and their religion, Theravada Buddhism, throughout Southeast Asia.

By the ninth century, the Bamar (Burmans), a subject people of the Pyu, had built a stronghold at Bagan, on the Ayeyarwady River. When the Pyu capital of Halingyi, in the dry zone, was destroyed by invaders from Nanchao (now Yunnan, in southwestern China) in the mid-ninth century, the Bamar became the dominant ethnic group in Myanmar.

Three Bamar Empires

Founded in A.D. 849, the first capital of the Bamar kings was Bagan. In 1044, King Anawrahta came to the throne. He defeated the Mon in 1057 and united the land under Bamar control. Anawrahta's dynasty became known as the First Burmese Empire. It lasted until the thirteenth century, when dwindling resources and Mongol invaders weakened the kingdom.

After the decline of Bagan, Myanmar was divided between the Mon and the Shan. The Mon made Bago their center and ruled southern Myanmar. The Shan moved from the highlands into central Myanmar, setting up their capital at Inwa.

The Bamar regained power in 1531 under King Tabinshweti of the Toungoo dynasty. Tabinshweti conquered the Shan from northern Myanmar and the Mon from southern Myanmar. With

the help of Portuguese mercenaries, he led wars against the Siamese (now Thai) and the Rahkine. In 1635, after crushing the Shan, the Bamar moved their capital to Inwa. In 1752, however, the Mon attacked and burned Inwa, ending the Second Burmese Empire. The same year, village headman Aung Zeya rallied the Bamar against the Mon and founded the Konbaung dynasty. Aung Zeya became King Alaungpaya. He attacked the Siamese kingdom and completely destroyed its capital, Ayuthia. He also conquered Rahkine and Taninthayi. During the reign of the Konbaung dynasty, British, Portuguese, Dutch, and French traders began to compete for control of the Southeast Asian sea trade.

Above: **The port of Yangon was an important trading center by the early nineteenth century, when Western interests in Myanmar began to intensify.**

The Anglo-Burmese Wars

In 1824, when Myanmar tried to conquer the territories of Assam and Manipur in neighboring British-controlled India, the British invaded Yangon. Myanmar was defeated in the ensuing war and forced to give up territories to the British. Some thirty years later, the British gained Bago and its surrounding areas in the Second Anglo-Burmese War. Finally, in 1885, the British captured the capital, Mandalay, in central Myanmar, bringing the Konbaung dynasty to an end. To the great shame of the people of Myanmar, King Thibaw and Queen Supayalat were wheeled out of the royal palace in an oxcart and were exiled to India.

British Administration and Nationalism

After the Third Anglo-Burmese War, the British sent about 30,000 troops and 8,500 military police officers to Myanmar, then called *Burma*. The country was ruled as a province of India, and the areas occupied by hill minorities were treated as "Frontier Areas," with British advisors assigned to the local rulers. The British brought peace and order to Burma and developed its economy, but the Burmese resented foreign rule. They felt that trade profits were benefiting foreign companies rather than Burma. Some Burmese

Above: **Baggage elephants and Indian attendants signaled the arrival of British officers in Mandalay in the 1880s. After three military campaigns, waged over a period of sixty years, the British annexed the whole of Myanmar to their empire in the East.**

THE KINGS AND THE "SHOE QUESTION"

As odd as it might sound, differences over the matter of wearing shoes signified larger cultural clashes and the breakdown of relations between the British and the Burmese during the nineteenth century.

(A Closer Look, page 58)

wanted to rule their country for themselves. In 1930, physician and former monk Saya San led a rural rebellion that took the British two years to suppress. In 1935, the Dobama Asiayone, or the "We Burmans" Association, was formed. Its members called themselves *thakin* (the-KIN) — Burmese for "master." The Burmese, who had long been forced to address the British as thakin, were now stating their position as the masters of their own country.

World War II and Independence

In 1940, the Thirty Comrades, a group of patriots led by nationalist Aung San, went to Japan for secret military training. They formed the Burma Independence Army (BIA) and invaded Burma with the Japanese in late 1941. Aung San was made commander-in-chief of the BIA. In 1943, the Japanese granted Burma independence in name but continued to rule in practice. Realizing they had been used, the leaders of the BIA made underground contact with the British, who had withdrawn to India. The BIA openly revolted in 1945 and helped the British drive the Japanese out of Burma. Aung San's negotiations with the British helped win independence for Burma in 1948. Aung San, however, did not live to see independent Myanmar. He was assassinated by gunmen under the command of U Saw, a former prime minister who opposed Aung San's leadership.

Left: **As Japanese soldiers advanced to Yangon (then called *Rangoon*) during World War II, they made use of native labor. The British, retreating into India, destroyed oil installations, mining equipment, and river transportation, hoping to slow the Japanese down.**

From Democracy to Military Rule

Myanmar became a republic on January 4, 1948. The first general election, held in 1951, was won by the Anti-Fascist People's Freedom League (AFPFL), a party founded by Aung San during World War II. Myanmar became a parliamentary democracy. By 1958, however, the AFPFL had split into two factions. In the years that followed, civil rule was threatened by armed clashes in villages and towns. In 1962, the army, led by General Ne Win, mounted a coup d'etat and arrested the prime minister, U Nu, along with several cabinet members and minority leaders.

General Ne Win set up a ruling Revolutionary Council consisting of senior military officers. All large businesses were nationalized. Pro-democracy demonstrations erupted through the

Left: **General Ne Win meets with peasants at a Peasants' Seminar in the 1960s. On April 30, 1962, Ne Win declared the Burmese Way to Socialism, a program of military dictatorship combined with state control of all economic enterprises. Ne Win resigned from the State Council in 1981, but he continued to be the chairman of the Burma Socialist Programme Party (BSPP) until 1988. The BSPP was the sole political party allowed to exist in Myanmar between 1964 and 1990.**

1980s, reaching a terrifying climax in 1988. General Saw Maung seized power, leading a brutal military crackdown in which thousands of unarmed demonstrators were killed. In 1989, *The Socialist Republic of the Union of Burma* became *The Union of Myanmar*, abandoning its socialist path. A government of army generals, called the State Law and Order Restoration Council, was formed, with Saw Maung as chairman and prime minister. Despite allowing multiparty elections in 1990, however, the military regime ignored the victory of the National League for Democracy (NLD), a coalition party headed by Aung San Suu Kyi and other opposition leaders. Today, Myanmar remains locked in this struggle between democratic and military elements.

Aung San (1915–1947)

Aung San is revered as a national hero and widely considered the father of independent Myanmar. Born on February 19, 1915, in central Myanmar, he was the youngest of six children. By 1936, he had made his name as a student leader at the University of Yangon. In the following decades, Aung San fought for Myanmar's independence, first against the British, then against the Japanese. He was assassinated on July 19, 1947, less than six months before Myanmar was granted independence from Britain.

Aung San

U Nu (1907–1995)

As a student, U Nu participated in university strikes organized against the British. An associate of Aung San, U Nu became Myanmar's first prime minister in 1948, after Aung San was killed. He led the AFPFL to victory in the 1951, 1956, and 1960 general elections. In 1962, however, the military seized power and imprisoned U Nu and many other leaders. Released in 1966, U Nu fled to Thailand, where he tried to organize opposition to General Ne Win. In 1980, when Ne Win announced an amnesty, or pardon, for his political opponents, U Nu returned to Myanmar. The government placed him under house arrest from 1989 to 1992 for his political activities.

U Nu

Aung San Suu Kyi (1945–)

Aung San's only daughter and the youngest of his three children, Aung San Suu Kyi was educated in Yangon, Delhi, and at Oxford University. She worked at U.N. offices in New York and Bhutan. In 1988, she returned to Myanmar to look after her dying mother and soon helped form the NLD. Fearing her popularity, the military government placed her under house arrest from 1989 to 1995. Since her release, her movements have been restricted, but she remains at the forefront of opposition to Myanmar's military regime. Aung San Suu Kyi was awarded the Nobel Prize for Peace in 1991. She has also received the Thorolf Rafto Prize for Human Rights from Norway and the Sakharov Prize for Freedom of Thought from the European Parliament.

Aung San Suu Kyi

Government and the Economy

Military Rule

The current military government imposed martial law (law established by the armed forces in response to civil unrest) on Myanmar in 1988. The 1974 Constitution and the state, divisional, township, ward, and village councils all were abolished. Although martial law was officially revoked in 1992, some of the decrees issued under the state of emergency are still in effect today. Three acts — the Emergency Measures Act, the State Protection Law, and the Unlawful Associations Act — allow the government to harass or detain government opponents. The State Protection Law was used to put opposition leader Aung San Suu Kyi and former prime minister U Nu under house arrest.

The current head of state is General Than Shwe, who is also the prime minister and the chairman of Myanmar's nineteen-member ruling military group, the State Peace and Development Council (formerly called the State Law and Order Restoration Council).

Above: **Yangon is the political center of Myanmar. This picture shows City Hall.**

THE HUMAN RIGHTS STRUGGLE

The government of Myanmar has come under severe international criticism for its treatment of political dissidents and minority groups.
(A Closer Look, page 54)

Armed Forces

The Tatmadaw, Myanmar's armed forces, number more than 320,000 and are the second largest in Southeast Asia, after Vietnam's. The army is grouped into twelve regional commands and ten light infantry divisions. Myanmar has twenty-three military intelligence companies working in urban areas and close to its borders, near Bangladesh, India, and China, to control political dissent. In addition, the police force numbers about 50,000. The People's Militia, a network of village-based groups, has about 35,000 members. The navy and air force have a combined strength of about 25,000.

Divisions and States

Myanmar is divided into seven divisions and seven states. The divisions — Ayeyarwady, Magwe, Mandalay, Bago, Yangon, Sagaing, and Taninthayi — are inhabited mainly by ethnic Bamar. The states belong to the larger minority groups: the Chin, Kachin, Kayin (Karen), Kayah, Mon, Rahkine, and Shan. Minorities such as the Kayin and Shan also live in areas outside the borders of their own states. States and divisions consist of smaller administrative units called townships, which are made up of villages and wards.

THE WAR AGAINST DRUGS

Myanmar is one of the largest opium-producing countries in the world. The government of Myanmar is doing its best to curb drug abuse and the illegal drug trade.
(A Closer Look, page 72)

Left: **General Than Shwe inspects the Royal Guard-of-Honor during a welcoming ceremony at Parliament Square in Kuala Lumpur, Malaysia, in 1996. Southeast Asian countries, such as Malaysia, Singapore, and Thailand, have a policy of "constructive engagement" with Myanmar, although many Western countries strongly oppose the dictatorship of the military regime.**

A Struggling Economy

After Myanmar gained independence in 1948, the government reversed the liberal economic policies of the British, who had encouraged exports and foreign investment in new businesses. By the 1980s, however, falling export prices and rising national debt had become major problems. Economic reforms to encourage foreign investment and liberalize trade have met with limited success. Today, Myanmar's economy remains one of the least developed in Southeast Asia. The majority of the workforce is employed in the agricultural sector. Common cash crops include beans, corn, rice, groundnuts, sugarcane, sesame seeds, and a range of fruits and vegetables.

Below: **Agriculture is the backbone of Myanmar's economy.**

The Black Market

A black market, or illegal trade in goods, develops when there is an acute shortage of certain goods. In 1962, when the military came to power, the government took over the distribution of essential goods, such as rice, cooking oil, and gasoline. Demand was overwhelming, however, and government shops often had bare shelves. The black market developed to supply these goods. Today, smuggled goods are sold openly in ordinary markets, alongside crafts and other legal products. Black-market goods consist of food, textiles, medicine, cosmetics, household items, electrical merchandise, and transportation equipment. Currency is also exchanged. On the black market, U.S. currency is worth more than fifty times its legal value.

URBAN CENTERS

Although Myanmar is largely a rural country, urban centers, such as Yangon, Mandalay, Mawlamyine (Moulmein), and Pathein, are well developed and relatively modern.
(A Closer Look, page 66)

Resources, Trade, and Industry

The large-scale extraction of Myanmar's rich mineral deposits began in the 1970s. Deposits of lead, silver, and zinc have been found in the northern part of the Shan Plateau. Tin and tungsten are found in Taninthayi. Myanmar also has small reserves of oil and natural gas. International oil companies have been offered energy concessions for exploration.

Myanmar's main exports are rice, teak, minerals, and gems. Before World War II, Myanmar was the largest rice exporter in the world. Today, however, Myanmar has fallen behind the United States, Thailand, China, Vietnam, India, and Bangladesh. Myanmar is one of the world's richest sources of teak, but its teak

VALLEY OF RUBIES

Northeast of the city of Mandalay lies the gem-producing valley of Mogok.
(A Closer Look, page 68)

Above: **Ships dock at Yangon's port on the Hlaing (Rangoon) River.**

forests are rapidly being depleted. Other hardwood trees include pyinkado (Burmese ironwood), padauk, kanazo, and bamboo. Consumer goods, machinery, and industrial raw materials make up the bulk of Myanmar's imports. The country's main trading partners are the European Union, Japan, China, India, Singapore, and Malaysia.

The state owned all industries from 1962 to 1977, when some light industries were privatized. The current military government still controls the teak, petroleum, natural gas, gemstone, and banking sectors. Today, 9 percent of Myanmar's labor force works in manufacturing industries, the largest of which is the food and beverage industry. Other industries include construction materials, minerals, and petroleum products.

People and Lifestyle

The government of Myanmar recognizes about 135 ethnic groups in the country. About 70 percent of the population is descended from the Bamar, who arrived from Central Asia and Tibet before the fifteenth century. Apart from the Chinese and Indians, most minority ethnic groups live mainly in the hills. The hill peoples' lifestyles and languages are distinct. Some are Buddhists or Christians, but many still adhere to their traditional practices of worshiping local spirits. They have always tried to remain independent of the Bamar kingdoms and have fought many wars to preserve their separate cultures.

Minority Groups

Consisting of about 8.5 percent of the population, the Shan from Shan state are the largest minority group in Myanmar. The term *Shan* covers thirty-three ethnic subgroups in Shan state, including the Padaung, Intha, Danu, and Palaung. Their language, T'ai, is closely related to the languages spoken in northern Thailand and Laos. Predominantly farmers, the Shan grow irrigated rice, tea, and temperate fruits and vegetables.

The Kayin make up about 6.2 percent of the population and consist of many subgroups. Many Kayin are Christians. Other

Left: Burmese of all ages often apply a yellowish paste, called *thanaka* (th'-nah-KAH), to their faces. Thanaka is made from the bark of a flowering shrub belonging to the citrus family. The bark is ground into powder, and water is added to form a paste. Thanaka has a light, natural scent and is said to prevent sunburn and protect the skin against oiliness.

HILL MINORITIES

Shan state is home to several hill tribes, including the Palaung and the Akha.

(*A Closer Look, page 50*)

ethnic minorities in Myanmar include the Mon from Mon state in southern Myanmar and the Rahkine from Rahkine state in the western part of the country. Although the Mon and Rahkine share a common language and religion with the Bamar, they historically had independent kingdoms and fought many wars against the Bamar.

The Burmese Way

The Burmese pride themselves on proper etiquette. Public displays of excessive emotion, whether prompted by anger or by love, are frowned on. Elders and others of a higher status, such as monks, should be addressed and treated with courtesy. It is considered rude, for instance, to pass things over the heads of seated elders. To show respect to grandparents, parents, and teachers on formal occasions, the Burmese kneel down with their foreheads and elbows touching the ground. When passing a pagoda or meeting a monk, they put their palms together in a gesture of reverence.

Burmese people are also very sensitive about imposing on, or inconveniencing, other people. The fear of embarrassing others is called *anade* (AH-nar-DEH). If you asked a Burmese guest what drink you could serve him or her, your guest would probably say, "Anything is fine," to avoid embarrassing you by asking for something you might not have.

Below: Women of the Padaung ethnic minority are famous for their neck rings. First worn at an early age and increased as the girl grows older, the rings on an adult can weigh up to about 20 pounds (9 kilograms)!

Close-Knit Families

Burmese households often consist of three generations. If family members do not live in the same house, they usually live near each other and visit often. Children learn to share and to participate in family life at an early age. Siblings and cousins often share bedrooms. Children take part in all social occasions, apart from funerals. In rural areas, they often run small errands for adults or help out in the fields. All children are expected to respect and obey not only their parents but all their elders. They are also expected to take care of their aged parents.

Above: **As soon as they are old enough to walk, many children accompany their parents on social visits and, in rural areas, even to work in the fields.**

Men and Women

In Buddhism, men have a higher status than women — Buddhists believe in reincarnation, and a woman has to hope that, in her next life, she is reborn as a man.

The husband is considered the spiritual head of the Burmese household because of his *hpon* (PONE), or spiritual status. In public, women let men take the lead, often walking behind their husbands or fathers. At home, however, a husband usually hands his earnings over to the wife, who manages the family budget and often runs her own small business, too.

Women are excluded from certain areas of religious buildings, such as the middle platform of the Shwedagon Pagoda. Despite the hierarchy of Buddhism, however Burmese women have a quiet self-confidence that comes from a tradition of independence. At a time when many women in other parts of the world had no legal rights, a Burmese woman could choose whom to marry, even if her parents disagreed. She could divorce her husband by putting her case before the village elders, and, if her complaints were fair, her request would be granted. Today, just as in the past, a woman keeps the money and property brought into a marriage. If she divorces, she keeps not only what was hers before marriage but also her share of any money or property in the family business. Women also have equal rights of inheritance with men. They dominate the markets as traders of goods or food vendors. Today, there are many women in professional occupations, too, working as doctors, dentists, lawyers, writers, teachers, and scientists. At universities in Myanmar, female enrollment equals that of males.

Below: **Women of Amarapura carry their wares to market. More than a century ago, Sir George Scott, a British colonial officer, wrote that a "married Burmese woman is much more independent than any European, even in most advanced states."**

Going to School

Myanmar has a high literacy rate, and just as many girls as boys attend school. Children enroll in kindergarten at the age of five. At the age of six, they progress to Standard 1. From kindergarten to the second standard, they learn Burmese, English, and arithmetic. At Standards 3 and 4, their academic subjects include geography and history, and, from Standards 5 to 8, the children also study science. In Standards 9 and 10, the school curriculum expands to include biology, civics, and economics. A national examination is taken at the tenth standard. Schools also offer religious education in Buddhism.

The average school day starts at 9 a.m. and ends at 3 p.m., with a forty-five-minute lunch break. Some schools have two sessions, with students in the first session starting and finishing earlier than in single-session schools, to make room for afternoon-session students.

The dropout rate in Myanmar is high — only 25 percent of schoolchildren go beyond Standard 4. In rural areas, especially, children tend to leave school at a relatively young age, to help in family businesses.

Below: School-children in Mandalay work hard at their lessons. Education is compulsory between ages five and nine.

Higher Education

For Burmese who remain enrolled in school, higher education is a priority. Diplomas and degrees not only help in getting jobs but also bring prestige.

Entry to universities is very competitive — only one in five applicants is selected. University placement is allocated according to examination results at the end of Standard 10. Students with the highest aggregate scores pursue medical degrees. Those with the next best results enter dentistry, engineering, veterinary science, agriculture and forestry, economics, education, science, and the humanities, in that order. The University of Yangon and the University of Mandalay are Myanmar's oldest institutions of higher learning.

In the past, the military government has met with considerable opposition from dissident student groups. Due to student unrest, Myanmar's universities have been closed since 1996. Today, many students from well-to-do families attend universities in countries such as Thailand, Singapore, Australia, the United Kingdom, and the United States.

Above: Schoolchildren in Yangon welcome the rainy season with smiles.

THE JOB MARKET

Like many other developing countries, Myanmar has a large pool of highly educated people who are unemployed. Since the private sector is small, most jobs are provided by the state, but graduates far exceed the number of positions available. Many educated Burmese leave their country to find work in Europe, North America, and other parts of Asia.

Buddhism: The Four Noble Truths

Almost 90 percent of Myanmar's population practices Buddhism, a major religion with some 300 million followers worldwide. Its two main branches are the Theravada and Mahayana doctrines. While Theravada Buddhism focuses on individual enlightenment, the Mahayana tradition seeks to bring salvation to all humans. Almost all Bamar, along with a large proportion of minority groups, are Theravada Buddhists.

Buddhism began about 2,500 years ago. *Buddha* means "Enlightened One" and refers to northern Indian prince Siddharta Gautama (c. 563–483 B.C.). Prince Siddharta left a life of privilege

Below: **Buddhist nuns make their way to a temple.**

to wander the world as a poor, religious man in search of the meaning of life. After many years of seeking and a period of intense meditation, he finally reached a peaceful state of mind that was free from all worldly desires. Buddhists call this plane of existence *nirvana*, or the state of Enlightenment.

The essence of Buddhism is contained in the Four Noble Truths — that all life involves suffering; that such suffering comes from desire or greed for things or people; that this suffering can stop if people learn to live without desire; and that this enlightenment, or detachment from worldly things, can be achieved only by following the Eight-Fold Path, or Middle Way, a philosophy that avoids extremes and emphasizes good deeds.

EARNING MERIT

Burmese Buddhists are very concerned about earning religious merit through good deeds. The highest form of merit making for a family is the *shin-byu* (shin-BYEW) ceremony, when a boy becomes a monk for a temporary period.
(A Closer Look, page 46)

CHRISTIANITY

Western missionaries brought Christianity to Myanmar hundreds of years ago. They found more converts from among the hill minorities than among the ethnic Bamar, who are staunch Buddhists. Today, most Christians in Myanmar are Baptists, a legacy of active American Baptist missions in the last two centuries. Yangon has two cathedrals, St. Mary's Cathedral *(left)* and St. Paul's Cathedral.

Because doing good is thought to bring the believer closer, stage by stage, to nirvana, all Buddhists try to keep the Five Precepts, or rules of conduct — not to lie, steal, kill (even insects), take intoxicants (such as alcohol or drugs), or commit sexual misconduct.

Other Beliefs

Myanmar's Muslim population is concentrated in Rahkine state. The hill minorities worship various kinds of spirits, such as forest spirits, and their beliefs vary from group to group. These spirits differ from the *nat* (NAHT) spirits, or wandering souls, worshiped by some Burmese.

HONORING THE SPIRITS

Every year, nat worshipers hold several ceremonies, the most important of which is the Taungbyon Festival.

(A Closer Look, page 52)

Language and Literature

The Burmese language belongs to the Sino-Tibetan family of languages. Burmese script was originally adapted from the Mon language. Both scripts were derived from Pali, the ancient Indian language of the sacred text of Theravada Buddhism.

Almost all early Burmese writing was religious. Before printing became common, the Bamar wrote in stone and on palm leaves, using a sharp metal point. Modern Burmese has undergone many changes and is substantially different from the Old Burmese of ancient stone inscriptions, some of which date back to the eleventh century.

The Burmese language has thirty-three consonants and twelve vowels. Like Thai, Vietnamese, and Mandarin, Burmese is a tonal language. Its four tones are partly differentiated by pitch and by stops at the end of syllables. Words with the same syllables but different tones can have entirely different meanings.

Colloquial Burmese — the everyday, spoken form of the language — differs from literary Burmese in certain aspects of grammar and vocabulary. Literary Burmese is used in official documents, newspapers, textbooks, and news broadcasts. Attempts at transliteration, or writing Burmese in English letters according to the way it should be pronounced, have not been very successful, because English cannot reproduce all the sounds used in the Burmese language.

Literature

Although the people of Myanmar love to read, books are relatively scarce because the country is poor. Imported books are expensive, and Myanmar has only about three hundred public libraries. All locally printed work, including fiction, has to be submitted to censors who follow the military regime's strict guidelines on what can be printed. Writers and cartoonists have been imprisoned for their perceived criticism of the regime. Despite these restrictions, however, Myanmar's writers produce many fine works of fiction, culture, and the arts and sciences.

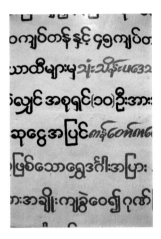

Above: **The Burmese script is derived from the ancient Pali language of India and Ceylon (now Sri Lanka). Most of the minority groups in Myanmar speak their own languages, along with Burmese as a second language.**

NAMES AND TITLES

The Burmese have no last names or family names. Each person has an individual name, and a woman does not change her name at marriage. Titles and formal terms of address are used to show respect — men have their names prefixed with *U* (OO), which means "uncle," and women are addressed as *Daw* (DAW), or "aunt." Only friends may omit these polite terms of address.

Ma Ma Lay (1917–1982)

Myanmar's most distinguished woman writer, Ma Ma Lay, was born Ma Tin Hlaing, in 1917, in Bogalay, a small town in the rice-growing area south of the Ayeyarwady delta. Under the pen name of *Gyanegyaw Ma Ma Lay*, she contributed articles to the newspaper *Gyanegyaw*. She also wrote works of fiction. Her novel *Thulo Lu* (*A Man Like Him*), written after the death of her husband in 1947, was an outstanding literary achievement. In 1948, she became chairperson of the National Writers' Association of Myanmar.

Ma Ma Lay's works criticized all forms of injustice. In late 1963, she was arrested and detained for three years for allegedly helping a former defense minister and friend of the nationalist hero Aung San to escape. Ma Ma Lay's novel *Not Out of Hate* is the first Burmese novel to be published in English outside Myanmar. Her novel *Thwei* (*Blood*) was translated into Japanese and voted the best foreign novel of the year. She received the award in Japan in 1980.

Below: **An alternative to the public library is the book rental shop, or *sa-ok-hnga-hsaing* (sar-oak-HNGA-sayng), which rents out the latest novels and magazines.**

Arts

Myanmar has an established artistic tradition. Its pagodas boast elaborate friezes, wall paintings, and sculptures. Local art forms, such as marionette theater and *kalaga* (kah-lah-gah) making, are internationally renowned. Myanmar's hill minorities also have distinctive arts and crafts.

Marionette Theater

Marionette performances were a popular form of entertainment in eighteenth-century Myanmar, before the British took control of the country. At their peak in the nineteenth century, marionette shows were more popular than live theater and received royal patronage. Today, however, overtaken by videos and movies, marionette theater is a dying art form.

Traditionally, the puppets are about 22–27 inches (56–69 centimeters) tall, with up to eighteen strings. Performances are based on stories from the *Jataka*, the sacred text that recounts the Buddha's many incarnations, or past lives.

Below: **A puppet troupe consists of puppeteers, singers, and an orchestra. The success of the troupe depends more on the talent of the lead singer than on the skill of the puppeteers. The audience comes not only to watch the show but also to listen to and appreciate the poetry of the lyrics.**

Left: **Kalaga are long pieces of embroidered cloth made of silk, cotton, wool, or velvet and decorated with appliqued trees, flowers, animals, or scenes from the *Jataka*. The designs are padded with cotton wool and hand-stitched with glass mosaics, silver sequins, pearls, and other precious stones.**

Kalaga

Lengths of kalaga, or richly embroidered cloth, were traditionally used as portable curtains by monks, royalty, and rich people. Kalaga pieces could be attached, with ropes, to trees, posts, or pillars to create an enclosed, private area. The art of kalaga making declined rapidly after the British took over Myanmar and abolished the monarchy. Many old pieces of kalaga were donated to monasteries or bought by collectors. Some beautiful pieces are now housed in museums outside Myanmar. The art of kalaga making was kept alive by Burmese classical drama, whose dancers and marionettes wear kalaga costumes. In the 1970s, tourism helped revive the craft. Today, kalaga pieces are made mainly for export and come in varying shapes and sizes.

Parabaik

Made of paper, *parabaik* (pa-ra-BIKE) are folding picture books measuring up to several yards long. Brightly colored illustrations recount the Buddha's life and depict the Bamar royal court, as well as ordinary people, animals, and buildings. Parabaik are meant to be viewed panel by panel from left to right, so that the scenes follow in order. When not in use, parabaik are kept folded and stored in special manuscript chests.

LACQUERWARE

Myanmar's lacquerware artisans produce beautiful items for everyday and decorative use.

(A Closer Look, page 60)

Gold Leaf

Gold leaf is traditionally used to gild items — such as lacquerware, musical instruments, religious images, and manuscript storage chests — for royal or religious use.

Mandalay is the center of the gold leaf industry in Myanmar. In the manufacturing process, small lumps of gold are pounded into thin strips, then heated and flattened in a machine. The resulting sheets are repeatedly hand-beaten, then cut into small squares, placed between sheets of special paper, and wrapped in animal skin. Beaten again until they are no thicker than a layer of paint, the gold sheets are cut into squares of about 2 inches (5 cm), sandwiched between sheets of special paper, and sold in bundles.

Pwe

Pwe (PWAIR) is a popular form of entertainment that combines music, drama, and dance. There are many kinds of pwe — *zat pwe* (ZAHT PWAIR), adapted from the *Jataka*, portrays the Buddha's lives; nat pwe is enacted for various spirits worshiped by some

LAND OF PAGODAS

Myanmar is dotted with incredible pagodas, from the splendid Shwedagon to the mysterious Golden Rock *(above)*.

(*A Closer Look, page 62*)

Left: **Buddhist worshipers press thin squares of gold leaf onto Golden Rock (Kyaiktiyo Pagoda). It is considered an act of merit to gild religious images and objects.**

32

Left: **The boat-shaped Burmese harp has thirteen strings. The harpist sits and supports the instrument on his or her lap.**

Burmese; and *anyeint pwe* (ah-NYEINT PWAIR) is a musical comedy featuring clowns, jugglers, slapstick acts, and songs. Pwe are usually accompanied by dancers and a traditional orchestra, with the actors reciting their lines in verse.

Music

Traditional Burmese music is based mainly on percussion. Various kinds of music, songs, and dances are named after the kinds of drums used. Large *sidaw* (see-daw) drums are used for formal music, long *bonshee* (bone-shay) drums for folk music, and pot-shaped *ozi* (OH-zee) and two-faced *dobat* (DOE-baht) drums for village celebrations. Other instruments include oboes, flutes, gongs, cymbals, bamboo clappers, and bamboo xylophones.

The Burmese orchestra includes a drum circle of nine to twenty-one drums suspended on a circular wooden frame. A gong circle of up to nineteen gongs is arranged in scale on a wooden frame around a single performer. Western instruments, such as violins, guitars, and accordions, sometimes accompany the traditional instruments.

MODERN THEATER

Developed in the 1930s, *pya-zat* (pya-ZAHT) is a musical with a simple plot and little or no dancing. Unlike traditional theater, actors in pya-zat performances speak in colloquial prose. Today, the plays are performed to a paying theater audience.

Leisure and Festivals

In a country where radios are still more common than television sets, popular leisure activities often center around free outdoor public events, such as festivals and pwe. Visiting friends, going to the movies, and taking part in outdoor sports are also popular pastimes.

Traditional Theater and Film

Myanmar's traveling theater, or pwe, groups perform outdoors, at temporary venues or on simple bamboo stages. Performances often last throughout the night and might continue for several days. In the countryside, the audience usually sits on the ground on thin grass mats.

Although the country hosts a small film industry, Myanmar imports most of its films, typically action-packed blockbusters. All local film scripts must be government approved. Most locally produced films are based on love stories and, like pwe, feature plenty of singing and dancing.

Below: **Subtitled Indian movies are very popular in Myanmar.**

Children's Games

Burmese children are adept at making toys from old household items. Catapults, used to fire pellets of dried mud, are made using strong Y-shaped twigs and rubber bands. Avid kite fliers add an extra thrill to their hobby by coating their kite strings with glass powder and using them to sever their opponents' kite strings in airborne "fights." Children practice their origami (paper folding) skills by cleverly turning bits of paper into boats, birds, and boxes.

Children also play many kinds of group games. In *kyet-hpa-hkut-tan* (CHET-hpa-koot-tun), or "the Cockfighting Game," players sing a rhyme about cockfighting while imitating the movements of cocks. They continue these actions until a player loses balance, falls over, and is out of the game. The winner is the child who can keep up the actions longest. Another game is *kyet-pyan-nghet-pyan* (CHET-pyahn-NGHET-pyahn), or "Hens Fly, Birds Fly." Seated in a circle, children take turns naming an object. If a flying animal or object is named, the other players have to raise both of their hands. Anyone who makes a mistake is out of the game.

Above: **Burmese children never run short of inventive finger and hand games.**

Boxing

Burmese boxing has no specific rules, except that the boxer is not allowed to bite or scratch the opponent or kick him in the groin. The winner is the boxer who draws blood for a fourth time, after the opponent has been allowed to wipe away blood three times.

Rowing

Traditional boat races take place all over Myanmar during some festivals that are held in the rainy season. On Inle Lake, the boat races are unusual because the rowers propel their boats standing up, with one leg wrapped around an oar.

Above: **A fisherman on Inle Lake demonstrates his one-legged rowing technique.**

Chinlon

Chinlon (CHIN-LONE) is a Southeast Asian game played with a rattan or cane ball measuring about 4 inches (10 cm) in diameter. The purpose of the game is to keep the ball in the air, using only feet, knees, elbows, shoulders, or heads — but not hands! The game can be played alone or with others standing in a circle. Two teams can also pit their skills against each other in a game similar to volleyball. This game is enjoyed by women as well as men, and Chinlon associations have been established all over Myanmar.

Below: **Chinlon is a simple sport that requires only a rattan ball.**

Left: **The bloody sport of cockfighting is taken seriously by many enthusiasts in Myanmar.**

Other Rural and Urban Sports

In the countryside, villagers organize traditional cockfights, with spectators laying bets on the bird they hope will win. Bird owners sometimes attach sharp spurs to the legs of their roosters, which are trained to attack the opponent. These contests draw large, cheering crowds.

In cities such as Yangon, people enjoy the kinds of sports popular in other parts of the world — golf, tennis, badminton, basketball, volleyball, and track and field events. Soccer, judo, karate, and *thaing* (THINE), a Burmese martial art and form of self defense, all are popular throughout the country.

Above: Crowds gather for a drenching during Thingyan, the Water Festival, in mid-April.

Festivals

In Myanmar, a festival takes place just about every month, often on the day of the full moon. Some festivals are celebrated across the country. Others, such as local nat festivals or the unveiling of a new pagoda, are regional. National holidays include Independence Day on January 4, National Day on the twenty-fifth day of Tazaungmone (October/November), and Christmas on December 25.

Thingyan

Thingyan, or the Water Festival, takes place toward the end of the hot, dry season and ushers in the Burmese New Year. The festival lasts three to five days. Standing on bamboo stages erected along the streets, people splash water on passersby. Powerful water pipes douse people driving by in jeeps and trucks. Children use water pistols to drench their friends, relatives, and anyone else in range — only monks and the elderly are safe! The water symbolizes the washing away of the previous year's bad luck and sins. On New Year's Day itself, all the water-throwing ends. This day is celebrated by releasing captive fish and birds as acts of merit, and special feasts are held for monks.

CALENDAR DIFFERENCES

Both the Burmese and Buddhist calendars are based on lunar cycles. While the Burmese calendar lags some 638 years behind the Western, or Gregorian, calendar, the Buddhist calendar is charted from the year the Buddha attained nirvana. The year A.D. 2000, therefore, corresponds to the Burmese year 1362 and the Buddhist Era 2544–2550.

From Lent to the Weaving Festival

The Waso Robe Offering Ceremony marks the beginning of the three-month Buddhist Lent in the month of Waso (June/July). This ceremony celebrates the Buddha's first sermon, delivered forty-nine days after he attained nirvana. During the ceremony, monks are offered robes to wear during Lent, a time when they are not allowed to travel. No weddings, feasts, or festivals are celebrated during the Buddhist Lent, and people try to follow the Five Precepts more conscientiously.

The end of Lent is marked by the Festival of Lights in the month of Thadingyut (September/October). Houses and state buildings in Myanmar are ablaze with lanterns, candles, or electric bulbs. Young people show their respect for elders by formally presenting them with gifts of food or longyi.

The Weaving Festival is celebrated between October and November, in the month of Tazaungmone. Monks are, again, offered robes, and feasts are held for merit-making. At the Shwedagon and other pagodas, all-night weaving contests take place, in which participants race to finish weaving robes for the Buddha images by dawn.

HARVEST FESTIVAL

The festival of *hta ma-ne* (tah m'-NEH) celebrates the rice harvest in the month of Tabodwei (January/February). A tasty rice pudding (hta ma-ne) is made from glutinous rice, peanuts, ginger, sesame seeds, and shredded coconut. The sticky mixture is stirred in huge pans, then divided into small amounts, wrapped in banana leaves and distributed to monks and guests.

Below: Shin-byu novitiates join the New Year's Day festivities in Bagan.

Food

Fruits and Vegetables

Myanmar is blessed with a mind-boggling array of fruits and vegetables. The huge jackfruit can weigh up to 80 pounds (36 kg) and measure up to 3 feet (1 m) in length! Its yellow, fibrous flesh is sweet, and even its seeds can be eaten, boiled or roasted. The durian is an olive-green, spiky fruit about the size of a soccer ball. Few can be indifferent to its pungent smell, which inspires extremes of love or loathing! The custard-like flesh is nutritious, containing iron, and Vitamins B, C, and E. Other popular fruits include avocados, mangos, pineapples, papayas, bananas, rambutans (hairy red or yellow fruits), mangosteens, watermelons, pomelos (large tropical citrus fruits), and custard apples. Among the many vegetables Burmese enjoy are okra, eggplant, and water spinach, a green vegetable with hollow stems and tapering leaves.

Cooked Food

Burmese food reflects the influence of Myanmar's two main neighbors, India and China. Many of the spices used, particularly in curries and spicy snacks, originated in India. Ingredients such as bean curd, condiments such as soy sauce, and culinary

Left: **Meat and vegetable fritters are sold at streetside food stalls all over Myanmar.**

techniques such as stir-frying reveal Chinese influence. Chinese-style snacks, such as spring rolls and meat buns, are also readily available in Myanmar.

Burmese dishes rely on an assortment of spices — tamarind, chili, garlic, coriander leaves, and lemon grass — to bring out the flavor of the food. Fish sauce and fish paste are also used commonly, and coconut milk is an important ingredient in desserts.

Lepet is a specialty made of pickled tea leaves marinated in oil and crushed garlic. Lepet plays an important part in traditional Myanmar society and is customarily eaten by two people who accept the decision of a village elder in settling their complaints. Lepet is also offered to visitors, nibbled by tired students trying to stay awake, and enjoyed by people watching pwe through the night.

Eating in Myanmar

Many Burmese eat their meals at low, round tables, sitting on the floor on mats. All the dishes are placed on the table and are eaten at the same time, not course by course as in the West. In some homes, meals are served at Western-style tables and are eaten with spoons and forks. Most people, however, eat with their fingers.

Above: **Most Burmese eat with their fingers instead of with utensils. The left hand takes food from the serving dishes to the plate, and the right hand is used for eating off the plate. Rice, boiled in water or coconut milk, is a staple. The most common drink in Myanmar is tea, which is grown in Shan state.**

A CLOSER LOOK AT MYANMAR

Myanmar is a land of natural beauty and cultural splendor. This section presents a few of the enchanting places in Myanmar — Inle Lake with its floating markets and villages, the fertile plains of the Ayeyarwady delta, the disappearing teak forests of the minority highlands, and Mogok, the famous valley of rubies. Myanmar's many pagodas illustrate the religious devotion of the Burmese. Buddhist traditions survive today in pilgrimages to pagodas and in other merit-earning customs.

The people of Myanmar have a proud history. The archaeological site of Bagan is a monument to the success of the

Opposite: **Yangon's Shwedagon Pagoda is one of Myanmar's most important Buddhist shrines.**

ancient Bamar kingdom. The Bamar monarchy lasted for several dynasties before the British won full control of Burma in the Third Anglo-Burmese War of 1885.

Today, battles of a different kind are being waged in Myanmar. Hill minorities, such as the Shan, Kayin, Palaung, and Akha, have maintained their traditions and continue to assert their identities against dominant Bamar rule. The military government faces opposition from dissidents alleging human rights abuses and calling for greater political freedom. The government also battles illegal drug production in Myanmar.

Above: **Horse- or ox-drawn wagons and carriages are a common form of transportation, especially in rural Myanmar.**

Bagan's Ancient Splendor

Situated on the eastern bank of the Ayeyarwady River in central Myanmar, the ancient Bamar capital of Bagan has been described as a place of "exquisite ruins." Two thousand pagodas, large and small, occupy 16 square miles (41.4 square km) of scrubland. Only two other archaeological sites in Southeast Asia — Cambodia's Angkor Wat and Indonesia's Borobodur — rival the architectural magnificence and beauty of Bagan.

A Golden Age

Founded in about A.D. 849, Bagan served as the first Burmese royal capital from 1044 until 1287. It was a center of Theravada Buddhism, the religion practiced in Myanmar and promoted by King Anawrahta in the eleventh century. The art and architecture of Bagan owed much to the Mon. Anawrahta brought some 30,000 Mon monks, artisans, and scholars to Bagan as part of his war booty from the conquest of the Mon. At the height of the empire

Below: The ruins of ancient pagodas dot the scrubland. More than one thousand years ago, the forests of the Bagan region were cut down for firewood, used to bake bricks for these pagodas.

in the eleventh century, about five thousand temples stood in Bagan, their architectural styles ranging from early Indian and Mon to later, typically Burmese styles.

The period of Bagan glory is now also considered the golden age of Burmese art. Although the Bamar constructed other buildings, such as teakwood palaces, monasteries, and libraries, only Bagan's breathtaking pagodas remain standing today. The Shwezigon Pagoda, built by King Anawrahta, ranks with the Shwedagon in Yangon and Phaung Daw U on Inle Lake as one of the most important shrines in Myanmar. The cross-shaped, 170-foot (52-m) Ananda Temple houses four 30-foot (9-m) standing Buddha statues. At 190 feet (58 m), the Thatbyinnyu holds the distinction of being the highest temple in Bagan.

In 1287, Bagan was sacked by the invading armies of Kublai Khan from China and, later, it was attacked by the Shan. An earthquake on July 8, 1975, further destroyed many of the temples. A few have since been restored, but some landmark structures, such as the 900-year-old Buphaya Pagoda, were lost forever.

Today, in the small communities around Bagan and in the neighboring village of Nyaung U, people make their livings by fishing, weaving, and producing lacquerware.

Above: **The impressive Shwesandaw Pagoda in Bagan was restored after the devastation of the 1975 earthquake.**

Earning Merit

Leading Good Lives

Buddhists believe that to reach the plane of spiritual existence
called *nirvana,* a person must be reborn and live many lives, each
a little better, hopefully, than the one before. Meditation and
prayer count as good deeds. Other commendable works include
almsgiving, worshiping in pagodas, shrines, or at altars, and
acting generously without expecting any return in this life.
Because earning merit is so important, many Buddhists give food
to monks and nuns, hold feasts to feed lots of guests, and donate
money to repair or build pagodas or resthouses.

Bringing Honor to Others

One person's kind or noble act can also earn merit for someone
else. In the past, wealthy people gave land, money, and even
servants to monasteries. These temple servants earned merit for
their former owners as well as for themselves. Similarly, when a
boy or young man joins a monastery, that act brings honor to his
whole family. For this reason, the shin-byu ceremony, or initiation
into temporary monkhood, is a significant rite in Burmese culture.

Above: **Buddhists
in Amarapura offer
food to the monks in
their town. This is
considered an act
of merit.**

Shin-byu: The Making of a Monk

Shin-byu is a religious ceremony that all Buddhist boys are expected to undergo. It is considered the highest merit-earning act for the family. During the ceremony, would-be monks, or novitiates, are dressed in fine clothes to imitate the Buddha's early life as a prince. The boys are then carried, paraded on a horse, or taken in a car around the neighborhood. Their families hold elaborate feasts. Then comes the head shaving rite, which symbolizes giving up a life of luxury. A boy's parents usually hold out a white towel to collect his hair as his head is shaved. Newly shorn novitiates say prayers in Pali with monks, then enter a monastery, usually only for a few days or a week — shin-byu monkhood is temporary. At the monasteries, the novitiates learn to meditate, read the Buddhist Scriptures, and do humble tasks, such as sweeping the premises and running errands for the monks. Shin-byu is so important in Burmese cultural life that families without sons occasionally "adopt" nephews, male cousins, or other boys to hold the ceremony. Towns and villages sometimes hold mass ceremonies, during which up to one hundred boys are initiated.

NUNS

Many Buddhist girls shave their heads and take temporary ordination as nuns. They choose this retreat to gain spiritual merit. They stay in convents for seven to ten days, going out to collect alms and experience being at the mercy of people's goodwill.

Below: The shin-byu ceremony is a proud occasion for the entire family. After a procession *(left)* and a feast, would-be monks have their heads shaved, sometimes by fellow novitiates *(right)*.

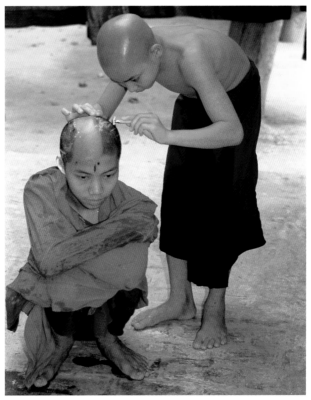

47

Getting Around in Myanmar

On Land

Myanmar is a largely rural country, with only about 100,000 road vehicles (cars, trucks, and buses) serving a population of about 44 million. Most modern vehicles are concentrated in the cities.

In isolated, mountain regions, life today remains much as it has been for centuries — people walk or rely on horse- or ox-drawn carts for transportation. In towns and cities, such as Bagan, Mandalay, and Pyin U Lwin (Maymyo), people also travel on bicycles and in trishaws (three-wheeled passenger vehicles pulled by bicycles attached to the side).

About 17,150 miles (27,594 km) of roads wind through Myanmar, but only about one-fifth of these roads are paved. Long journeys are usually made by train. Approximately 3,150 miles (5,068 km) of railroads link some five hundred train stations, and trains transport millions of passengers across the country each year.

BY AIR

Myanmar has nineteen airports. Myanmar Airways International, the country's international airline, offers direct flights from Yangon to Singapore, Bangkok, and Hong Kong. Two other airlines, Air Mandalay and Yangon Airlines, provide domestic flights.

Below: Traveling by bus in Amarapura is definitely not for the uninitiated!

By Water

Although not the fastest form of travel today, river transportation has always been important for ferrying goods and people within Myanmar. The Ayeyarwady, Myanmar's main river, is navigable for most of its length. Flowing from the northernmost regions of Myanmar to the Andaman Sea, the Ayeyarwady was greatly traveled by traders, especially before roads enabled easier access to much of the country.

The Ayeyarwady, its delta, and smaller river systems, such as the Chindwin, are still used frequently today. The Ayeyarwady has nine mouths — its delta includes some 2,000 miles (3,218 km) of navigable water. The Chindwin is navigable for about 400 miles (644 km). The inland waterways of Myanmar carry some 27 million passengers and about 3 million tons (metric tons) of cargo each year. Myanmar's main ports — Yangon, Pathein, Mawlamyine, and Sittwe (Akyab) — facilitate trading along the coast and with other countries.

Above: **Boats have been navigating Myanmar's rivers for most of the country's history. Oarsmen and ferryboat captains are adept at steering around sandbanks that shift rapidly in the dry season.**

Hill Minorities

The Palaung

One of the oldest hill groups, the Palaung live in the northern parts of Shan state. Their language, which consists of several dialects, is related to the Mon language. Many Palaung also speak the Shan language.

Palaung women stand out among the other hill groups for their colorful traditional dress. Their garments include velvet jackets of green, blue, or purple and longyi fastened with belts. Black caps, long, brightly colored hoods, and cloth leggings complete the outfit. Some women wear a different kind of headdress made up of colorful bands of cotton.

The Palaung are famous for the tea they grow and cure to sell, particularly the pickled tea, or lepet, popular with the Bamar and Shan. Palaung tea is grown on plantations at an altitude of about 6,000 feet (1,829 m). Young tea leaves are picked, then steamed, rolled, and dried in the sun to produce green tea. In the pickling process, baskets of green tea leaves are placed in pits,

Below: **A Palaung woman brews the tea for which her people are famous.**

Left: The Akha are mainly farmers. They live in thatch-roofed houses with raised, wooden floors.

covered, and allowed to ferment. This process can last from a month to a year — the longer the fermentation period, the better the tea.

The Akha

Numbering several thousand, the Akha, or Kaw, are the second largest minority group in Shan state. They live in the mountainous areas east of the Thanlwin River.

Akha villages are easily identified by elaborate wooden gateposts carved with small figures of people and animals. These gateposts — a pair at either end of the village — separate and protect the village from the surrounding forest, where the Akha believe nature spirits roam. Like the dwellings of most other hill groups, Akha houses are made of wood and bamboo, with heavy, thatched roofs and wooden floors raised above the ground on posts. Each village is looked after by its own council of elders, usually the heads of households or their sons. The elders make important community decisions and elect the village priest and the headman.

AKHA STYLE

Traditional Akha clothing is decorated with silver details, applique, and embroidery. Women typically wear headdresses with patterns that vary according to subgroup. They also favor necklaces made of glass beads or seeds.

Honoring the Spirits

Left: **During a nat festival, villagers in Amarapura hold a procession to raise money for a new temple.**

Many Burmese believe that the souls of people who have died violently or from illness continue to wander on Earth. These spirits are called *nat.* Mahagiri, one of the thirty-seven "official" nat, is regarded as the most powerful of the spirits. He is worshiped at Mahagiri shrine on Mount Popa, an extinct volcano near Bagan. Hundreds of regional nat are also worshiped in different areas — nat of trees, rivers, and mountains, and guardian nat of homes and villages. Not all Burmese, however, worship nat. Some consider it superstitious and contrary to Buddhism. In the past, a few Burmese kings tried, unsuccessfully, to ban nat worship in the country.

Nat Pwe

Regional ceremonies in honor of the nat typically last several days and take place at temples, in homes, or on the streets. Bamboo shelters are put up for public shows known as *nat pwe.* A nat singer and an orchestra entertain the worshipers, who come to offer green coconuts and huge bunches of bananas to the nat. Other gifts to the spirits include cigarettes, alcohol, and perfumes. The central figure of the festivities is the *nat kadaw* (NAHT ka-daw), or nat-wife, a medium who enters a trance during the ceremony. Nat kadaw are usually women or transvestites (men who dress as women).

The Taungbyon Festival

The most important nat festival takes place at Taungbyon, near Mandalay, three times a year — in the months of Nadaw (around December), Wagaung (around August during the Buddhist Lent), and Tabaung (around March). Hundreds of nat kadaw and thousands of worshipers descend on Taungbyon during the festival. Trains are specially scheduled to transport the crowd from Mandalay, and the road to Taungbyon is jammed with traffic.

The Taungbyon nat festival lasts between five and fifteen days, with daily celebrations — drinking, dancing, and revelry —extending through the night. Homage is paid to the Taungbyon Brothers, an influential duo killed by King Anawrahta in a plot by palace enemies in the eleventh century. Besides typical nat offerings, worshipers present the Brothers' favorite food, wild rabbits.

Below: **Nat kadaw and worshipers present offerings at the main center for nat worship, Mahagiri shrine, on Mount Popa.**

The Human Rights Struggle

Many governments around the world cite Myanmar's poor human rights record, particularly in the rights to fair trials, freedom of expression, and fair treatment for minority groups. Under the dictatorship of the military, thousands of people have been unfairly imprisoned, including students, writers, political cartoonists, doctors, film producers, and members of the opposition party, the National League for Democracy (NLD). In 1988, antigovernment demonstrations in Myanmar made international headlines when hundreds of demonstrators were shot and killed by the military. In the 1990 general election, the government ignored the landslide 80-percent victory of the NLD.

Local outcry against this injustice has been largely silenced by tight regulation of speech and writing. Myanmar has only two television stations, one radio station, and one national newspaper (written in Burmese and English). The government controls this newspaper as well as Myanmar's three other local papers. Relatively few households have television sets, and even fewer

Left: **Aung San Suu Kyi, seen here with her aides, delivers a weekend speech at the gate of her house in Yangon. She was placed under house arrest by the military government from 1989 to 1995.**

have satellite television because the licence fee is exorbitant, at 12,000 *kyat* (CHAHT), which is approximately U.S. $2,000. The Press Scrutiny Board censors any written work, including books, magazines, song lyrics, and film scripts, that is interpreted as criticism of the government.

Minority groups in Myanmar have, from time to time, fought against the government for self-rule or independence. One government strategy has been to relocate the groups from their own villages to other areas, often with no choice and little warning. Those who resist are sometimes shot by the army as "insurgents" or "rebels." More than 20,000 people from Kayah state and about 300,000 people from 1,400 villages in Shan state have been made to move in recent years.

Forced labor is another serious problem in Myanmar. In minority areas as well as other rural regions, village headmen are often required to provide villagers as free labor to the government for a certain period of time. These workers, including women, children, and the elderly, are unpaid, badly treated, and sometimes even beaten. In towns, laborers may be plucked at random off the streets, trains, and ferries. Corrupt army officials often allow potential laborers to bribe their way out of work.

Many countries, including the United States, Britain, Sweden, and Japan have protested against the abuse of human rights in Myanmar. The European Union currently bans the sale of weapons to Myanmar.

Above: **The military crackdown on pro-democracy demonstrations in 1988 left thousands of protesters dead.**

FIGHTING FOR MYANMAR

Human rights and NLD leader Aung San Suu Kyi was married for twenty-seven years to British academic Dr. Michael Aris. Together, they helped raise international awareness of the plight of political dissidents in Myanmar. Dr. Aris died of cancer in 1999, not having seen his wife since 1995. Despite his illness, the government of Myanmar refused to grant him a visa to visit his wife. Aung San Suu Kyi chose not to leave the country, fearing she would not be allowed back in.

Inle Lake

Surrounded by mountains, villages, and several monasteries, picturesque Inle Lake measures about 10 miles (16 km) in length and about 4 miles (6.4 km) across.

Floating Markets and Artificial Islands

The largest village on Inle Lake is Ywama. Each of its two-story houses has its own landing dock, and boats are kept at the lake level. Every five days, a "floating market" brings buyers and sellers together in small boats on the lake. The markets sell a wide variety of fresh fruits, vegetables, flowers, and tobacco. The produce is grown on "islands" made from dredged-up water plants covered with fertile mud and anchored by bamboo stakes to the bottom of the lake. Inle Lake also supports several cottage industries, including weaving, silversmithing, and cheroot (a large, dark cigar with open, untapered ends) rolling.

Below: **A colorful floating market makes its way down a canal to Inle Lake. Most of the 35,000 people living on and around the lake are Intha, an ethnic group related to the Mon. Other groups living in the region include the Shan, Pa-O, Kayah, and Danu.**

The fishermen of Inle Lake possess a special skill — they row without using their hands! The fisherman or rower stands on one leg at the back of a sampan (a flat-bottomed boat) and wraps the other leg around an oar, rowing with powerful leg strokes. Standing up, the rower can see and steer through the lake's tangle of water hyacinths and weeds. This style of rowing also frees the fisherman's hands for throwing his nets out across the water.

Above: **Boat races are popular throughout Myanmar during festivals, but one-legged rowing races are held only on Inle Lake.**

The Phaung Daw U Festival

On the full moon days and nights of the Burmese month of Tazaungmone (October/November), Inle Lake hosts a magnificent festival. The Phaung Daw U ceremony takes its name from a temple on Inle Lake that houses five gilded Buddha images, each about 8 inches (20 cm) high. The Buddhas are said to have been carved on the orders of King Alaungsithu of Bagan in A.D. 1144, from sandalwood given to him by nat spirits. In the Phaung Daw U festival, the images are carried around to the lake's villages on a large barge with a *karaweik* (ka-ra-WAKE) — the Burmese royal bird — at its prow. People who are not able to visit the pagoda can pay their respects to the touring Buddhas.

The Kings and the "Shoe Question"

The three Anglo-Burmese Wars raged through the nineteenth century. Although Britain's larger motive was the extension of trade routes from India through Burma and into China, cultural differences were also responsible for the deterioration of relations between the two powers.

The First Anglo-Burmese War broke out in 1824, when Burma invaded neighboring Indian territories under British control. The war ended in 1826, with Burma losing the territories of Arakan (Rahkine today) and Tenasserim (Taninthayi today) to the British. This settlement did not remove mutual distrust between the Burmese and the British. In the early 1850s, British merchants accused Burmese officials of extortion. The British government in India sent naval officer Commodore Lambert to resolve the dispute, but the "Combustible Commodore," as historians have nicknamed him, had little tolerance or understanding of the Burmese. When his talks failed, Lambert blockaded Rangoon (Yangon, today), and destroyed several Burmese warships. War erupted in 1852, and the British annexed Pegu (Bago, today).

It fell to Burmese King Mindon, crowned in 1853, to negotiate peace. In 1862, the province of British Burma was formed by merging the three acquired divisions of Arakan, Tenasserim, and Pegu. King Mindon was also persuaded to accept a British Resident (an official advisor), Dr. Clement Williams, at the capital in Mandalay. Williams got along well with the king, and, in 1867, Mindon signed a treaty allowing British expeditions from Bhamo, in northeastern Burma, into western China.

For a time, Mindon's reign brought better relations with the British, but cultural differences were soon to resurface. In the 1870s, a border dispute arose between King Mindon and a minority hill tribe. The British sent Sir Douglas Forsyth to negotiate for the independence of the minority group. On Forsyth's return from Mandalay, he protested against the indignity of having to remove his shoes and sit on the floor before Burmese royalty. British officials, eager for the takeover of the remaining independent part of Burma, decreed that British

Above: **A fervent Buddhist, King Mindon ordered the Buddhist Scriptures engraved on 739 marble slabs and placed around the Kuthodaw Pagoda in Mandalay.**

Residents were to keep their shoes on in the royal presence. Angered by what he saw as flagrant disregard for Burmese customs, Mindon refused to receive any Resident in person. This loss of direct contact between British and Burmese representatives escalated the slide into war.

After King Mindon died in 1878, his successor, Thibaw, further alienated the British by cultivating French interests to balance British power. Thibaw treated his rivals ruthlessly, and court massacres led to the withdrawal of British Residents from Mandalay and Bhamo. Meanwhile, minority rebellions rocked northern Burma and Shan state.

British traders begged the government in India to intervene and end the unrest in Burma. The perfect chance came when Thibaw levied a huge fine on the Bombay Burmah Trading Corporation, a British teak company, for alleged illegal operations in Burma. Thibaw refused British demands to reopen the case for fair reassessment. The differences illustrated by the so-called "Shoe Question" culminated in the final breakdown of relations between the two powers. War operations began on November 14, 1885. Just two weeks later, British troops occupied Mandalay.

Left: **British troops arrived in Mandalay in 1885. The Third Anglo-Burmese War brought the whole of Burma under British control. Thibaw's humiliating surrender — he and Queen Supayalat were evicted from the palace in an oxcart — marked the end of the Konbaung dynasty and of the Burmese monarchy.**

Lacquerware

Historians believe that the art of lacquerware originated hundreds of years ago in Siam (Thailand, today) and spread to China before reaching Myanmar. Today, the oldest and largest lacquer industry is based in Bagan, in central Myanmar. Other lacquerware centers include Mandalay, Ywama on Inle Lake, and Kengtung (a town in Shan state).

Above: **In Bagan, lacquerware artisans produce elaborate pieces ranging from jewelry boxes and serving trays to furniture.**

What Is Lacquer?

Lacquer is a light, waterproof, easily molded material painted on objects, such as boxes, bowls, umbrellas, musical instruments, statues, and furniture, to give the items an attractive, patterned surface and a glossy finish. The lacquer used in Myanmar is the sap of a wild tree (unlike the lacquer used in India and Europe, which is the secretion of an insect). The trunk of a mature lacquer tree can measure up to 6 feet (1.8 m) in circumference. The sap, tapped by making cuts in the tree trunk, is stored in airtight containers. Its natural color is black, but certain kinds of lacquer can also be stained red. The best lacquer in Myanmar comes from Shan state.

Objects of Art

Most lacquerware items have bases made from long, thin strips of bamboo coiled or woven into specific shapes. Lacquer can also be painted on wooden or metal objects. Plain lacquer is mixed with finely ground clay, with ash from teak sawdust, or with rice husks to produce lacquer for different layers. The lacquer is then painted onto the object. After each layer is applied, the lacquer is dried and polished. Each item can have several layers of lacquer. When the final layer has been applied, designs may be cut into the lacquer to reveal layers of color beneath. Gold leaf patterns may also be applied to the object's surface. A single piece of lacquerware takes between six months and two years to produce, depending on its quality. Fine lacquerware bowls are made with very thin bamboo strips interwoven with horsehair. Even after the final layers of lacquer are applied, the bowl remains so flexible that its sides, when pressed together, can bend without cracking.

Left: **The motifs on Burmese lacquerware are inspired by plants, animals, folklore, geometric patterns, and Theravada Buddhism. Common designs include the Burmese zodiac animals, such as the rat, lion, tiger, serpent, guinea pig, elephant, and mythical galon-bird (*shown here*). Lacquerware household products include trays, plates, rice bowls, food containers, and cosmetics and storage boxes. In monasteries and pagodas, there are lacquered books, doors, pillars, ceilings, furniture, alms bowls, Buddha images, and manuscript chests.**

Land of Pagodas

Myanmar's Most Sacred Shrine

Containing eight hairs of the Buddha, the gilded Shwedagon Pagoda is built around a shrine believed to be 2,500 years old. The pagoda was only 27 feet (8.2 m) high originally, but successive kings built it higher and higher. In the eighteenth century, a Mon king raised the spire of the pagoda and gilded it. In 1871, King Mindon added a new tier adorned with diamonds, rubies, and other precious stones. The dome of the Shwedagon Pagoda now rises to more than 300 feet (91.4 m) and is covered with 60 tons (m tons) of gold leaf!

Below: **This reclining Buddha adorns one of the smaller shrines around the terrace of the Shwedagon Pagoda. Each year, thousands of pilgrims make their way to the Shwedagon to pray.**

Defying Gravity

A spectacular sight meets visitors to Mount Kyaiktiyo in Mon state. Resting on the edge of a cliff is a golden boulder with a girth of 50 feet (15.2 m). A small stupa 18 feet (5.5 m) high is perched atop the boulder. The entire marvel — Kyaiktiyo Pagoda, or Golden Rock — is 80 feet (24.4 m) high. An important center for pilgrims, Kyaiktiyo Pagoda is said to contain one of the Buddha's hairs. The Burmese believe that the rock was placed on the mountain ledge, 2,500 years ago, with the help of nat spirits.

A Merit-Earning Pilgrimage

At the bottom of Mount Kyaiktiyo and all along the path to its summit are resthouses built by well-wishers. Vendors sell bamboo and cane crafts, traditional herbal medicines, and food and drinks.

The 10-mile (16-km) hike up the mountain takes about four hours and earns the pilgrim merit. Between October and March, during the dry season, thousands of worshipers make this climb, a trek lined with many nat shrines. The journey is strenuous, but the path affords beautiful views of the surrounding springs and forest. Porters can be hired to help carry the pilgrims' luggage — or the pilgrims themselves — in hammocks attached to bamboo poles. Children can be carried in cane baskets. Along

the way, many pilgrims collect water from certain springs in bottles to bring home, believing the water possesses the power to cure illnesses. When the pilgrims reach the top of Mount Kyaiktiyo, they chant and meditate through the night. From the summit, they have to cross a short bridge built over a deep chasm to get to the flat ledge on which the golden boulder stands. Along the journey up the mountain, many of the pilgrims buy squares of gold leaf to apply to the rock's surface. Over the years, the gold leaf has accumulated to form a thick layer of solid gold!

Above: In a land renowned for its thousands of pagodas, the appearance and legend of Kyaiktiyo Pagoda, or Golden Rock, intrigues tourists and nat worshipers alike.

River of Refreshment

The Ayeyarwady River flows right through Myanmar, from the mountains of the north to the river delta in the south. Its name, which means "river of refreshment," reflects the status given it as Myanmar's lifeline. The 1,300-mile (2,092-km) river was historically important as a source of water, for fishing, for irrigation, for transporting people and goods, and for floating teak logs to mill towns and ports. Royal capitals of the past were all located close to the Ayeyarwady. Yangon, the current capital, sits on the river delta.

Before the British administration, the Ayeyarwady delta belonged primarily to the Mon. It was thinly populated and thickly covered with mangrove swamps and forests of kanazo, a wood used for fuel. The area was infested with mosquitoes, wild animals, such as tigers, and poisonous snakes. The delta farmers grew rice, mainly for their own consumption. Any excess rice was sent upriver to the royal capital, from which it was distributed, as needed, to other areas of the country.

The British brought about a dramatic change from the mid-1850s onward. They encouraged rice growing on a large scale and

Below: **Boats ferry people, light vehicles, and goods along and across the Ayeyarwady River.**

made rice a primary export. To control the extensive flooding caused by heavy monsoon rains, the British built canals and constructed embankments. As thousands of Bamar from areas north of the delta and a number of Kayin from the mountains moved to the delta to cultivate rice, the area became the rice bowl of Asia. Paddy fields grew from about 500,000 acres (202,350 hectares) to 8 million acres (3.2 million ha) in the later half of the nineteenth century, and the delta population increased from one million to eight million.

The area continued to prosper until the worldwide economic recession of the 1930s caused the price of rice to fall dramatically. World War II further damaged rice production — many farm animals were killed and agricultural tools destroyed. Today, however, the delta supports Myanmar's two major ports, Yangon and Pathein, and is the wealthiest, most populous and most heavily farmed region in the country. The Ayeyarwady River continues to be a vital communication and transportation line, linking the delta to the rest of Myanmar.

Above: **Rafts of floating logs form a makeshift "pier" along the Ayeyarwady River bank.**

AYEYARWADY FACTS

The Chindwin is the Ayeyarwady's main tributary. In the south, the Ayeyarwady divides into nine mouths that wind through a vast delta. The river bears so much silt that the delta is expanding all the time.

Urban Centers

Yangon

Located on the Ayeyarwady delta, Yangon is the capital and largest city in Myanmar, with a population of about four million. Formerly called *Dagon*, it was renamed *Yangon*, meaning "end of strife," by King Alaungpaya in 1755. It was only when the British took over the country, however, that Yangon (named *Rangoon* by the British) became an important port and capital. Today, Yangon handles more than 80 percent of the country's foreign trade and is Myanmar's main road, rail, water, and air transportation center.

Above: Old, colonial buildings are juxtaposed with more modern architecture in downtown Yangon.

Mandalay

Mandalay is the second largest city in Myanmar after Yangon and is widely regarded as the cultural center of the country. Founded in 1857 by King Mindon, Mandalay was the last royal capital before the British occupied all of Myanmar and moved the capital to Yangon. Modern Mandalay is a business hub for the northern part of the country. About 60 percent of Myanmar's monks live in this city, making it, also, a center of religious activity. Traditional artisans based in Mandalay specialize in silver and gold works, woodcarving, marble sculpture, silk weaving, and kalaga making.

Mawlamyine

The capital of Mon state, Mawlamyine sits on the coast of Taninthayi, in tropical southern Myanmar. During British rule, it was an important teak port at the mouth of the Thanlwin River. Today, Mawlamyine is famous for its tropical fruits, such as durians and pomelos, and for its cuisine. Two famous pagodas are located in this city — the 150-foot (46-m) Kyaikthanlan Pagoda and the Uzina Pagoda, which contains an image of a reclining Buddha.

Pathein

Located about 100 miles (161 km) west of Yangon, the port town of Pathein is the capital of Ayeyarwady division and a center for rice export and fish and shrimp products. Pathein's deepwater harbor allows heavy freighters to dock and pass through. The town, which supports a population of a few hundred thousand, is also famous for its pottery and colorful handpainted umbrellas.

Below: To the left, along the Pathein waterfront, is the golden dome of the Shwemoktaw Pagoda, built by the Mon king Samuddaghosa many centuries ago.

Valley of Rubies

Located about 124 miles (200 km) northeast of the city of Mandalay, the valley of Mogok has been producing some of the world's finest rubies for well over a thousand years. Some historians believe the area's earliest inhabitants were the first to discover gemstones in Myanmar, about six thousand years ago. Today, Mogok itself is something of a gem in a largely rural, backward part of the country. Over centuries, the excitement of discovering rare, precious stones and the promise of commercial rewards lured a steady stream of hopeful miners and gem dealers to the valley. Close to 500,000 people now live in Mogok, and the town's businesses, services, and infrastructure have developed to meet their needs. Although other colored gems are mined in Mogok, rubies are the valley's most renowned treasures.

A Gem Economy

A typical day in Mogok begins well before the sun's first rays light up the valley. In town, food hawkers sell their wares

Below: Gravel containing ruby deposits is emptied into sluices. Running water washes the gravel away, while the ruby deposits sink to the bottom of the sluices.

Left: Gem markets in Mogok bring ruby buyers and sellers together.

in the streets, and children make their way to school. On the outskirts of town, in the mining areas, miners eat their breakfasts and begin preparing the mines by pumping out any stale water that accumulated overnight in the shafts or pits.

Most of the mines in Mogok are worked in the same labor-intensive way. Once ruby deposits are located, the area is cleared. Surface or shallow deposits are mined in a simple, open pit, while deeper veins or mountain deposits have to be mined with shafts or from tunnels blasted out of the mountainsides with explosives. Gravel that contains rubies is carried from these mines and emptied into sluices, which are long, sloping troughs. Water washes away the lighter gravel, and the heavier residue is caught in grooves along the bottom of the sluices. Miners scrutinize this residue for the glimmer of precious stones.

Rubies do not reach the market in their natural state. Most homes in Mogok have a small room or workshop where the stones are cut and polished. Some of the gems are first heat-treated in special ovens to enhance their color and transparency. Although gem shops dominate the businesses in Mogok, and several outdoor gem markets operate daily, the most beautiful rubies are not available in Mogok but in the larger cities, such as Yangon or Mandalay. The finest stones are also exported to other Asian countries, Europe, and North America.

ALL ABOUT RUBIES

Valued in the past for their alleged magical properties, rubies are the most valuable members of corundum, the gem family that also includes sapphires and other colored stones. The main ruby deposits occur in semi-opaque masses or in crystals, in Myanmar, Thailand, and Sri Lanka. Rubies vary in color from deep red to light rose and even violet. The most prized stones are almost transparent, with a brilliant color described in the gem industry as "pigeon-blood red."

Vanishing Forests

The large-scale export of forest timber from Myanmar is causing serious ecological problems. Myanmar has been accused of selling its resources "like fast food," destroying its forests at a rate of about 2,317 square miles (6,000 square km) per year.

Making up 10–12 percent of Myanmar's forests, teak trees produce a very hard and durable timber. Teak has been widely used in temples and buildings in India and Myanmar for more than one thousand years. Teak trees can reach a height of up to 150 feet (46 m), with a maximum girth of 6–8 feet (1.8–2.4 m), and may take up to 150 years to mature.

Below: **In many of Myanmar's forested areas, elephants are still used to transport logs.**

Myanmar's teak forests have been owned by the state since 1948, and the felling, milling, and marketing of teak is controlled by a state organization, Myanmar Timber Enterprise. The most obvious reason for the overharvesting of forest timber is the income provided by teak exports, but opponents of logging also point to political factors. The forested regions are home to many of Myanmar's hill minorities, including the Mon, Kachin, and Kayin, who have been fighting for independence from the government of Myanmar for years. Some people allege that by allowing roads to be built into the forested lands to provide access for logging, the government can better penetrate the rebel areas and strengthen its political hold over the hill minorities.

An Environmental Threat

Elephants were traditionally used to haul the timber to rivers, where the logs were lashed together to form rafts and floated to the ports. Logging companies, however, are now introducing modern equipment to remove timber more efficiently. As a result, the forests, which take very long to regrow, are sustaining greater damage. When other trees, such as the Burmese ironwood, or the pyinkado, are chopped down at the same time, the unprotected soil is prone to erosion and leaching, or the washing away of precious nutrients by rainwater.

Left: **Myanmar surpasses India, Thailand, Indonesia, and Sri Lanka as the world's largest producer of teak. Teakwood is used for railway cars, shipbuilding, furniture, flooring, and door and window frames.**

The War Against Drugs

The poppy is a cash crop grown (both legally and illegally) in Kayah state, eastern Kachin state, and most of Shan state. Poppy seeds are sown by hand in fields cleared from the forests in September and October. From December, the hard work of harvesting begins. Thousands of poppy fruits have to be picked to obtain a few pounds of opium. Cuts are made in the poppy pods to allow the sticky white sap to run. The pods are then left overnight for the sap to harden and turn brown. This gummy substance, known as raw opium, is scraped off the sides of the poppy pods, shaped into balls, and wrapped in leaves or bark for sale.

Left: **The pretty poppy plant is the unlikely source of potent, addictive drugs. The narcotic effects of opium, produced from the immature fruits of the opium poppy, have been known since ancient times and were described in Greek texts dating back to the first century A.D. In 1806, German chemist F. W. A. Sertürner isolated a new drug, morphine, from opium. Morphine is prescribed to relieve pain and induce deep sleep, but its harmful side effects range from physical deterioration to acute poisoning. Morphine can be converted into heroin, a drug so dangerously addictive that its manufacture is prohibited.**

Opium dealers buy raw opium from the growers at moderate prices and make it into a powder or further treat it. In illicit operations, the opium is refined into heroin and smuggled out of Myanmar or sold illegally. In the remote highland areas where poppy plantations are found, it is difficult to detect opium smugglers. The dense forests shield them from ground and helicopter surveillance. Raw opium is transported by carriers, trucks, and mule caravans, to small, mobile heroin refineries that can easily be camouflaged or dismantled to avoid discovery. In opium-growing areas, growers and smugglers often have the protection of private armies that do not support the government of Myanmar. These armies derive part of their income from taxing illegal opium growers in return for army loyalty.

Below: Opium smoking is a popular pastime, especially among the hill minorities that grow poppies. Because of smuggling and illegal dealing, the massive profits of the drug trade seldom reach the poppy growers.

The government of Myanmar has taken stern measures to stop illegal drug production. Laws passed in 1993 impose strict penalties on drug abusers and traffickers, from a three-year prison sentence for failing to seek medical attention, to the death sentence for illicit production and distribution of opium, heroin, or other narcotic drugs. Between November 1998 and March 1999, nearly 10,000 acres (4,047 ha) of illegal poppy plantations were detected and destroyed. Quantities of opium, heroin, and other stimulants were also seized from various parts of the country.

RELATIONS WITH NORTH AMERICA

Relations between Myanmar and the United States began in the early nineteenth century, with the arrival of the first Americans, mostly Baptist missionaries, in Yangon. American missionaries, such as Adoniram Judson and Dr. Gordon Seagrave, overcame cultural barriers and forged strong friendships with the Burmese, even learning to speak and write the Burmese language fluently.

In the twentieth century, North American involvement in Myanmar intensified. When the British were forced out of Myanmar by the Japanese during World War II, the so-called "Burma campaign," a plan to recapture the country, became a

Opposite: **In 1988, pro-democracy demonstrations in Myanmar were brutally suppressed by the military. The brutality attracted severe criticism from many countries, including the United States.**

focus for the Allied forces of Britain, the United States, the Soviet Union, and China.

From the 1950s to the 1970s, Myanmar preserved friendly ties with North America despite differences in political views. Since the 1980s, however, the U.S. government has increasingly voiced objections to Myanmar's harsh treatment of political dissidents and minority groups, and diplomatic relations have soured. American law now prohibits all new American investment in Myanmar.

Above: **The Flying Tigers were a squadron piloted by American civilian volunteers. They helped protect the Burma Road (a vital supplies route between Bhamo and western China) from Japanese forces during World War II.**

Adoniram Judson (1788–1850)

The first Americans in Myanmar were Baptist missionary Adoniram Judson and his wife, Ann. After arriving in Yangon in 1813, Judson spent half his lifetime in Myanmar, returning only once to the United States. Judson had to learn the Burmese language in order to spread the Gospel. However, he was not able to convert many Bamar to Christianity because they were staunch Buddhists. He had more success with the Kayin. By the time of Judson's death at the age of sixty-two, the American Baptist Mission had converted 267 ethnic Bamar and 7,750 Kayin to Christianity. The Baptist College in Yangon, the city's only missionary college, was renamed *Judson College*. In 1920, this college became part of the University of Yangon.

Above: American Baptist missionary Adoniram Judson compiled a Burmese–English dictionary and translated the Bible into Burmese.

Dr. Gordon Stifler Seagrave (1897–1965)

Dr. Gordon Seagrave was born in Yangon in 1897 into a missionary family whose links with Myanmar extended back more than a century. He trained as a doctor in the United States and returned to Myanmar in 1922, with his wife and daughter.

The missionary hospital at Namkhan in Shan state, where Seagrave worked, was a rickety wooden building, unfurnished except for twenty wooden beds. Seagrave and his staff provided invaluable medical care to residents of the area, who otherwise had no access to medication. The majority of Seagrave's staff came from the hill minority groups. Seagrave learned Burmese and a few minority languages in order to train them personally. In 1928, Seagrave and his wife, with the help of nurses and Chinese laborers, built their own 100-bed hospital, as well as three branch hospitals.

During World War II, when the Japanese invaded China and Southeast Asia, Seagrave joined the U.S. medical corps. He organized a chain of hospital stations for Chinese soldiers under General Joseph Stilwell, the U.S. commander in Southeast Asia. Seagrave ran a mobile surgical unit that flew to areas that needed medical help. Seagrave's hospital at Namkhan was bombed by the U.S. Air Force in the war because the Japanese were using it as a base. After the war, Seagrave and his staff rebuilt and extended the hospital.

Opposite: Dr. Gordon Seagrave, affectionately known as the "Burma Surgeon," attends to a patient in his hospital at Namkhan. Seagrave wrote three books describing his life in Myanmar: *Burma Surgeon, Burma Surgeon Returns,* and *My Hospital in the Hills.* After his death in 1965, his hospital was taken over by the government of Myanmar.

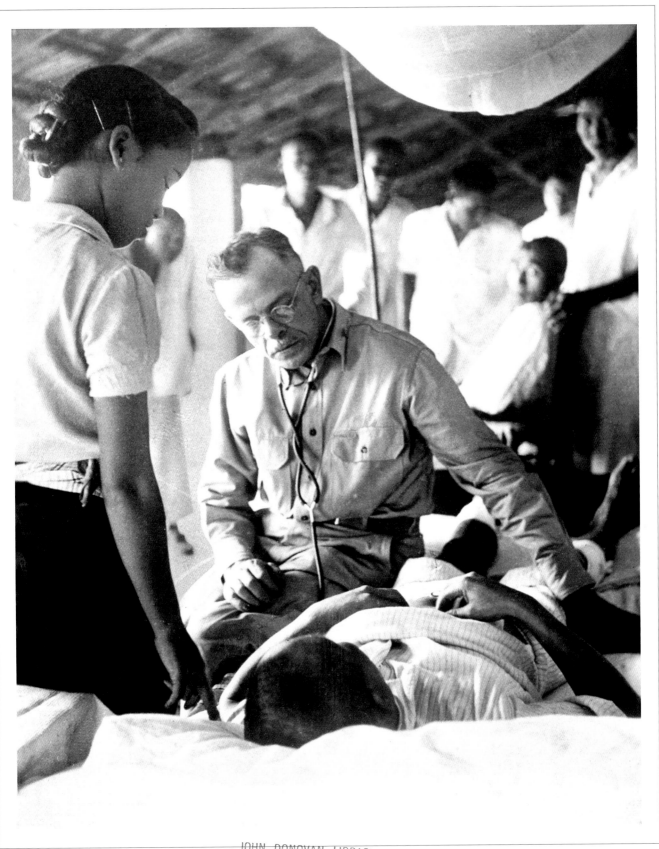

The Burma Road and the Flying Tigers

In 1937, after the Sino-Japanese War broke out and Japanese forces conquered the coast of China, the Chinese began constructing a highway connecting Lashio, in eastern Myanmar, to Yunnan province in China. Completed in 1939, the Burma Road covered a distance of 717 miles (1,154 km). For three years, it functioned as one of China's few links to the outside world, carrying vital supplies of food and weapons into the country.

When World War II broke out in the Pacific Theater in 1941, American forces fought hard alongside their Southeast Asian counterparts against the invading Japanese. From 1941 to 1942, a group of American civilian volunteer pilots, known as the Flying Tigers, defended the Burma Road and the Chinese capital of Chungking (now, Chongqing, in Sichuan province). Although outnumbered by the better equipped Japanese air force, the Flying Tigers destroyed many Japanese air and ground forces.

In April 1942, however, the Japanese seized Lashio and sealed off the Burma Road. The Flying Tigers, absorbed into the U.S. 10th

Below: **Along the mountainous China–Myanmar border, a woman from a minority group works on the Burma Road in 1944. After the Japanese sealed off the Road at Lashio in 1942, Allied forces created a route from India that joined with the China-controlled part of the Burma Road. This new road, opened in January 1945, allowed the Allies to send supplies to aid the war effort in China.**

Air Force, continued to fight for the Allies. Allied forces helped liberate Myanmar, and the Japanese were defeated in 1945. Today, the Burma Road still exists as part of a 2,100-mile (3,380-km) road system linking Yangon to Chongqing.

Above: **On February 21, 1961, Burmese staged a demonstration outside the U.S. embassy in Yangon. They protested the shooting down of a Burmese plane by a Chinese Nationalist plane on the Myanmar–Thailand border.**

The Cold War

The start of the Cold War, a period of nonviolent enmity between the Soviet Union and the United States over their incompatible systems of government, threatened to divide the rest of the globe into opposing pro- and anticommunist camps. China was split between communist rule on the mainland and the Nationalist government in U.S.-supported Taiwan. In 1953, 12,000 Chinese anticommunist troops fled from communist China into Myanmar. The Myanmar government feared that China would invade the country if it was thought to be harboring anticommunist elements. Following Myanmar's appeal to the United Nations, the United States deported half of the Nationalist troops to Taiwan. In 1961, however, anti-American riots broke out in Yangon and Mandalay over the discovery of American arms in the camps of the remaining Nationalist forces. Myanmar had to repeat its appeal before more Chinese Nationalists were evicted from the country.

The Nonaligned Movement

At a meeting in Bandung, Indonesia, in 1955, Myanmar was one of the twenty-nine founding members of the Nonaligned Movement, an organization of countries that wanted to remain neutral in the Cold War. As more countries joined the movement, it was difficult to agree on policies, and true nonalignment was elusive. Myanmar left the movement in 1979. After the end of the Cold War and the collapse of the Soviet Union in 1991, neutralism ceased to play an important part in many countries' foreign relations.

Overtures of Friendship

In 1955, Prime Minister U Nu of Myanmar visited the United States and was received by U.S. President Dwight D. Eisenhower and Secretary of State John Foster Dulles. U Nu thanked the United States for helping free Myanmar from Japanese occupation during World War II. He presented a check for U.S. $10,000 to American war veterans.

In 1962, when the military seized power in Myanmar, the country embarked on a policy of isolation. Nevertheless, General Ne Win visited the United States in 1966 and was hosted by

Above: **Drug smugglers use mules and horses to transport packs of raw opium to a heroin refinery close to the Myanmar–Thailand border in 1991. In the past, the U.S. has supplied surveillance helicopters and light aircraft to help the Myanmar government in its drive to detect and eliminate illegal poppy plantations and drug refineries.**

President Lyndon Johnson. The following year, the United States gave arms and ammunition to General Ne Win to fight communists in Myanmar.

Deterioration of Diplomatic Ties

Relations between the United States and Myanmar took a turn for the worse after 1988, when the military government killed many pro-democracy demonstrators and, in 1989, put politician and human rights leader Aung San Suu Kyi under house arrest. The government also refused to hand power over to the NLD despite its victory in the 1990 national election. In 1997, twelve American cities, one county, and the state of Massachusetts banned all contracts with companies that had dealings with Myanmar. Although the Foreign Trade Council, the European Union, and Japan challenged this ruling, in 1998, President Clinton banned all new American investment in Myanmar. At present, there is no U.S. ambassador in Myanmar. The U.S. diplomatic representation is headed by the Chief of Mission.

Below: A Buddhist monk prays at a vigil for Aung San Suu Kyi in London, England, in 1991. Many countries, including the United States, objected to the Myanmar government's treatment of Aung San Suu Kyi in the early 1990s.

U Thant and the United Nations

U Thant was born in 1909 in Pantanaw, a town in the Ayeyarwady delta area. He was educated at the University of Yangon and recruited into the civil service by U Nu and Aung San. In 1957, he was appointed Myanmar's Permanent Representative to the United Nations. He became the third Secretary-General of the United Nations five years later, a post he held for two terms, from 1962 to 1971. As Secretary-General of the United Nations, U Thant oversaw the transfer of Dutch-held Papua to Indonesia. He also helped ease tension between the United States and the Soviet Union over the discovery of Soviet missiles in Cuba. U Thant's other political achievements included negotiating a cease-fire in the 1965 Indo-Pakistan War and speaking out against the Vietnam War. U Thant died of cancer in New York City in 1974, at the age of sixty-five.

Visiting Myanmar

As a result of poor relations between the governments of Myanmar and North America, very few North Americans

Left: **Myanmar-born U Thant was the third Secretary-General of the United Nations. When he died in 1974, thousands of people went to the U.N. headquarters in New York to pay their last respects. Yet, in Myanmar, the military regime shocked the international community by not receiving U Thant's coffin with due respect and ceremony. Mass demonstrations by students, monks, and other U Thant supporters finally prompted the military government to relent. U Thant was buried in a private tomb in Yangon.**

Left: American artist Melanie Maung, who is half Burmese, lives in Boston, Massachusetts. She is part of a small number of second-generation Burmese-Americans. Melanie's father, the late Professor Mya Maung of Boston College, was a vocal critic of the Burmese military regime and a champion of human rights for the people of Myanmar.

currently live or work in Myanmar on a long-term basis. In the 1980s, tourists were issued only seven-day visas, and their movements were restricted to certain parts of the country. After the 1988 military coup, the number of tourists visiting Myanmar plunged from about 40,000 to 9,000.

Today, however, the government of Myanmar encourages group tours to the country. Visitors can now stay up to four weeks, but their destinations are limited, and journalists and human rights activists are still unlikely to be granted visas.

Living in North America

The Burmese population in North America numbers only about 100,000. The largest community lives in Los Angeles, California. Most Burmese immigrants to the United States arrived in the 1960s, in response to political repression by General Ne Win's military government. After the 1988 demonstrations in Myanmar, when the military imprisoned and killed many people, a large number of Burmese fled the country. Most went to Thailand, while others migrated to the United States, Australia, or other parts of Asia, such as Singapore.

Buddhism

The biggest Burmese cultural legacy in the United States is probably Theravada Buddhism. There are sixteen Burmese Buddhist temples in the United States. Half of these are in California. Temples have also been built in Illinois, Florida, Nevada, New Jersey, New York, Texas, and Maryland. Canada has two temples, one in Vancouver and the other in Toronto.

Since North America has no definitive Burmese cultural center, temples function as houses of prayer and meeting places for most Burmese-Americans and Burmese-Canadians. Some temples also offer Burmese language lessons and teach the Buddhist scriptures.

Important Buddhist festivals are celebrated at the temples. The most popular include the Thingyan (Water) Festival and robe-offering ceremonies. North American Burmese also celebrate the Festival of Lights and the Harvest Festival.

Preserving Burmese Culture

Burmese in North America have adapted readily to Western lifestyles. Most take on Christian names and wear Western-style clothing, keeping their traditional longyi for the home or for visits to temples or monasteries.

Left: **Buddhist monk Sayadaw U Pyinnya Thiha poses outside a temple in New Jersey.**

Above: **A Burmese-American boy has his head shaved as part of the shin-byu ceremony.**

The Burmese language is still spoken at home, especially among the elderly. Younger Burmese often understand the language, although they may not be able to speak or write it. There are no special Burmese language schools, although lessons are conducted at some temples.

Buddhist traditions are still widely practiced by many Burmese-American and Burmese-Canadian households. As in Myanmar, the shin-byu ceremony is regarded as an act of merit, and some boys bring honor to their families by undergoing it. Unlike their counterparts in Myanmar, however, North American monks do not "beg" for their food, because a non-Buddhist culture would not understand or support this religious activity. Instead, monks in North America rely on other Buddhists to bring them cooked food.

In 1981, the America Burma Buddhist Association was established in New York to preserve Burmese culture in the United States. The Association runs the Universal Peace Buddha Temple in New York and the Mahasi Retreat Center for meditation in New Jersey. The four-story temple in New York has a 4-foot (1.2-m) Buddha seated on a gilded teak throne.

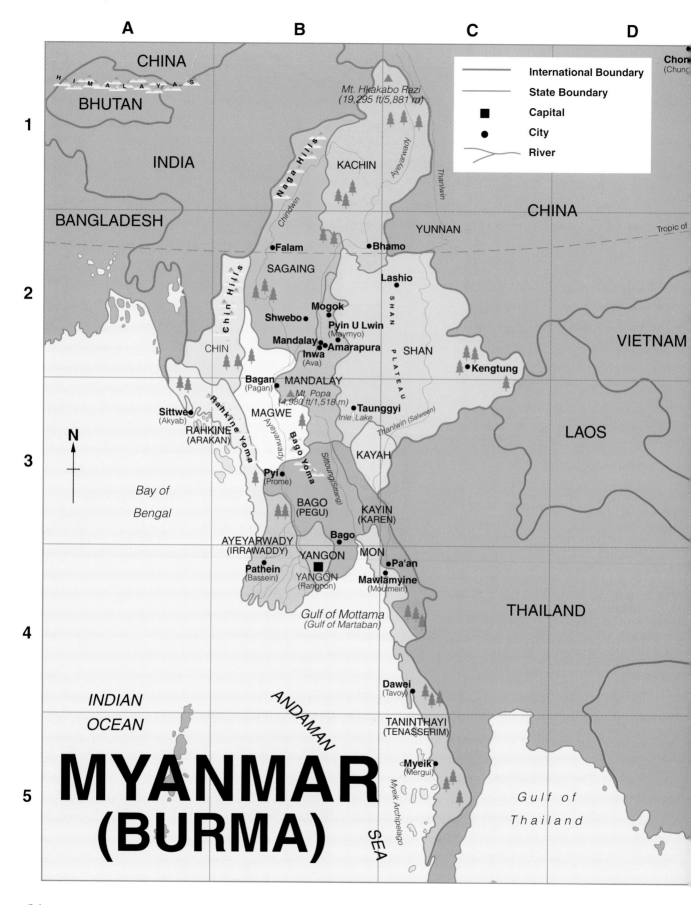

MYANMAR (BURMA)

Above: Workers tie sheaves of paddy in the rice fields of Amarapura.

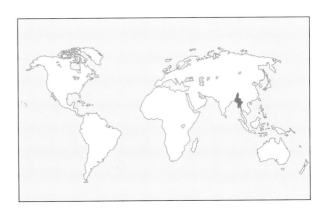

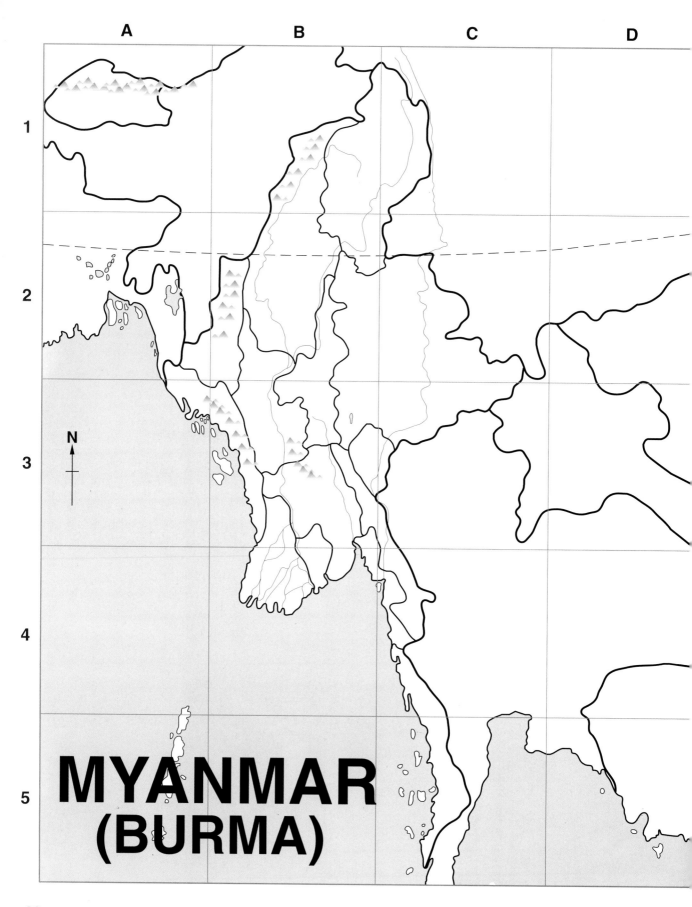

MYANMAR (BURMA)

N

A B C D

1
2
3
4
5

How Is Your Geography?

Learning to identify the main geographical areas and points of a country can be challenging. Although it may seem difficult at first to memorize the locations and spellings of major cities or the names of mountain ranges, rivers, deserts, lakes, and other prominent physical features, the end result of this effort can be very rewarding. Places you previously did not know existed will suddenly come to life when referred to in world news, whether in newspapers, television reports, or other books and reference sources. This knowledge will make you feel a bit closer to the rest of the world, with its fascinating variety of cultures and physical geography.

Used in a classroom setting, the instructor can make duplicates of this map using a copy machine. (PLEASE DO NOT WRITE IN THIS BOOK!) Students can then fill in any requested information on their individual map copies. Used one-on-one, the student can also make copies of the map on a copy machine and use them as a study tool. The student can practice identifying place names and geographical features on his or her own.

Above: **These young Buddhist monks live in a monastery on Inle Lake, in Shan state.**

Myanmar at a Glance

Official Name	The Union of Myanmar
Capital	Yangon
Official Language	Burmese
Population	44,305,319 (1998 estimate)
Land Area	261,228 square miles (676,580 square km)
States	Chin, Kachin, Kayah, Kayin, Mon, Rahkine, Shan
Divisions	Ayeyarwady, Bago, Magwe, Mandalay, Sagaing, Taninthayi, Yangon
Highest Point	Mount Hkakabo Razi at 19,295 feet (5,881 m)
Major Rivers	Ayeyarwady, Chindwin, Thanlwin (Salween)
Main Religion	Theravada Buddhism (89 percent)
Life Expectancy	53 years (men), 56 years (women)
Literacy	83 percent
Major Festivals	Buddha Day (Banyan Tree Watering Festival)
	Burmese New Year
	Festival of Lights
	Harvest Festival
	Kahtein Robe-Offering Ceremony
	Thingyan (Water) Festival
	Waso Robe-Offering Ceremony
Major Cities	Mandalay, Mawlamyine (Moulmein), Yangon
Flag	The flag of Myanmar bears a small blue rectangle on a red background. In the blue rectangle, surrounded by fourteen stars, are a cogwheel and a rice plant.
Currency	Kyat (K 6.25 = U.S. $1 as of 1999)

Opposite: **The Royal Palace in Mandalay.**

Glossary

Burmese Vocabulary

anade (AH-nar-DEH): in Burmese etiquette, the practice of showing consideration for others by not embarrassing them.

anyeint pwe (ah-NYEINT PWAIR): a musical comedy.

bonshee (bone-shay): a long drum used for folk music.

chinlon (CHIN-LONE): a Southeast Asian game played with a rattan or cane ball. The object of the game is to keep the ball in the air using any part of the body except the hands.

Daw (DAW): the formal Burmese term of address for a woman.

dobat (DOE-baht): a two-faced drum used in village celebrations.

eingyi (AIN-jee): a blouse worn by Burmese women.

gaungbaung (GOWN-BOWN): the turban-like headgear worn by Burmese men.

hpon (PONE): a certain spiritual quality or status that the Burmese believe men possess.

hta ma-ne (tah m'-NEH): tasty cakes traditionally made from glutinous rice, peanuts, ginger, sesame seeds, and shredded coconut.

kalaga (kah-lah-gah): a richly embroidered piece of cloth that was traditionally used for curtains.

karaweik (ka-ra-WAKE): the Burmese royal bird.

kyat (CHAHT): the unit of currency in Myanmar.

kyet-hpa-hkut-tan (CHET-hpa-koot-tun): "the Cockfighting Game," a children's game in which players sing a rhyme about cockfighting, while imitating the movements of cocks.

kyet-pyan-nghet-pyan (CHET-pyahn-NGHET-pyahn): "Hens Fly, Birds Fly," a children's game in which players take turns naming an object and differentiating between flying and non-flying objects.

longyi (lone-jee): a tubular skirt worn by men and women in Myanmar.

nat (NAHT): in traditional Burmese beliefs, the souls, or spirits, of people who have suffered violent or tragic deaths.

nat kadaw (NAHT ka-daw): a nat medium.

ozi (OH-zee): a pot-shaped drum used in village celebrations.

parabaik (pa-ra-BIKE): a religious picture book or manuscript.

pwe (PWAIR): a traditional form of entertainment or performance.

pya-zat (pya-ZAHT): a musical with a simple plot and little or no dancing.

sa-ok-hnga-hsaing (sar-oak-HNGA-sayng): book rental shops in Myanmar.

shin-byu (shin-BYEW) : an initiation ceremony into temporary monkhood.

sidaw (see-daw): a large drum used for formal music.

thaing (THINE): a Burmese martial art and form of self defense.

thakin (the-KIN): master.

thanaka (th'-nah-KAH): a light yellow paste made from the powdered bark of a flowering shrub. Thanaka is believed to be good for the complexion.

U (OO): the formal Burmese term of address for a man.

zat pwe (ZAHT PWAIR): a dramatic portrayal of the Buddha's lives, adapted from the *Jataka*.

English Vocabulary

amnesty: a general pardon for political offenses against a government.

annexed: added (as a territory) to the domain of a state, country, or empire.

camouflaged: hidden by being disguised to blend in with the surrounding environment.

coalition: a union into one organization.

colloquial: describing everyday or informal speech or writing.

coup d'etat: an unexpected political uprising.

delta: a flat plain that forms from the material deposited by a river at its mouth.

dissidents: individuals or groups who reject an established political authority.

embankments: banks or mounds raised along a river to prevent flooding.

exiled: expelled from one's native land.

ferment: to undergo a process of chemical change caused by organisms such as yeasts, molds, and certain kinds of bacteria.

flagrant: glaring; shockingly obvious.

friezes: decorative carved panels, usually at the tops of walls.

homage: respect; reverence.

house arrest: the confinement of a person to his or her home or to a public place instead of prison.

intoxicants: substances that severely alter physical and/or mental control.

latitude: the angle of a location on Earth, measured in degrees moving away from the Equator.

marinated: describing food soaked in a seasoned liquid (such as vinegar or oil) to add flavor before cooking.

marionette: a puppet controlled from above using strings attached to its jointed parts.

martial law: law imposed by state military forces in response to civil unrest.

monsoon: the seasonal wind of the Indian Ocean and southern Asia, blowing from the southwest in summer (wet monsoon) and from the northeast in winter (dry monsoon).

nationalism: devotion and loyalty to one's own nation.

nationalized: brought under the ownership of the state.

navigable: describing a body of water that allows ships or boats to pass through.

novitiates: persons admitted into a religious order.

privatized: transferred from state control to private ownership.

socialist: describing a theory or system of government in which the production and distribution of goods are controlled by the state or by all the people.

transliteration: the changing of letters and words from one alphabet or language into the corresponding characters of another alphabet or language.

More Books to Read

Aung San Suu Kyi: Fearless Voice of Burma. Newsmakers Biographies series.
Whitney Stewart (Lerner)

The Beauty of Fired Clay: Ceramics from Burma, Cambodia, Laos, and Thailand.
Hiromu Honda and Noriki Shimazu (Oxford University Press)

Burma. Cultures of the World series. Saw Myat Yin (Benchmark Books)

Burma: Encountering the Land of the Buddhas. Ellis Everarda (Weatherhill)

Burma: From Monarchy to Dictatorship. Aung Chin Win Aung (Yoma Publishing)

Burmese Dance and Theatre. Images of Asia series. Noel F. Singer (Oxford University Press)

Cultural Sites of Burma, Thailand, and Cambodia. Jacques Dumarcay and Michael Smithies
(Oxford University Press)

Faded Splendour, Golden Past: Urban Images of Burma. Oxford in Asia Paperbacks series.
Ellen Corwin Cangi (Oxford University Press)

In the Forest with the Elephants. Roland Smith and Michael J. Schmidt (Gulliver Books)

Myanmar Style: Art, Architecture and Design of Burma. Luca Invernizzi Tettoni, Elizabeth
Moore, and John Falconer (Periplus Editions)

Pagan: Art and Architecture of Old Burma. Paul Strachan (Weatherhill)

Videos

Mission of Burma: Live at the Bradford. (Video Music Inc.)

Mystic Lands — Burma: Triumph of the Spirit / Jerusalem: Mosaic of Faith. (Fox / Lorber)

Web Sites

www.geocities.com/TheTropics/Cabana/7789/burmanf.htm

planet.simplenet.com/Kiscadale/Pagan.htm

www.roadtomandalay.com/mmarinf.htm

nobelprizes.com/nobel/peace/1991a.html

Due to the dynamic nature of the Internet, some web sites stay current longer than
others. To find additional web sites, use a reliable search engine with one or more of
the following keywords to help you locate information about Myanmar. Keywords:
Aung San Suu Kyi, Ayeyarwady River, Bagan, British Burma, Mogok, Shwedagon, teak.

Index